BM7 (our)
MA office

INDIA
Past into Present

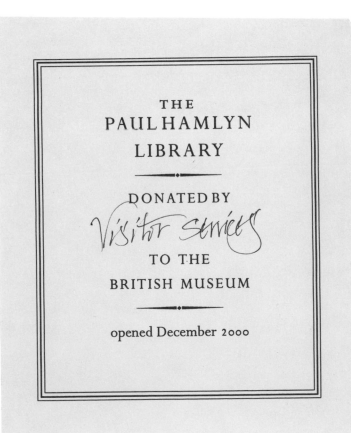

Brian Durrans & Robert Knox

INDIA
Past into Present

 Published for the Trustees of the British Museum by
British Museum Publications Limited

© 1982, The Trustees of the British Museum

Published by British Museum Publications Ltd,
46 Bloomsbury Street, London WC1B 3QQ

British Library Cataloguing in Publication Data

Durrans, Brian
   India: past into present.
   1. India – History
   I. Title
   II. Knox, Robert
   95H   DS436

   ISBN 0–7141–1422–7

Designed by Harry Green

Set in VIP Palatino
and printed in Great Britain by
Fakenham Press Limited,
Fakenham, Norfolk

Page 1 A railing cross-bar from the stupa at
      Amaravati depicting a scene of
      elaborate court life with nobles
      entertained by a large group of female
      dancers and musicians. BM 1880. 7–9. 12.
      (See also p. 46.)

Page 3 Embroidered cotton *toran*, traditionally
      pinned above a door for good fortune.

Front cover Traditional bullock cart, beneath a
      banyan-tree in Vasna, with
      modern tyres.

Back cover A bullock cart incised on a jar from
      Inamgaon, *c.* 1300 BC.

Contents

Acknowledgements   *page* 6

Preface   7

PART ONE
From village to city in ancient India
Robert Knox   9

1 Introduction   11

2 Rural bias   13

3 The first settlements   15

4 Neolithic villages   18

5 Village to city   24

6 Return to the villages   35

7 Iron Age and early cities   39

8 The later monasteries   49

PART TWO
Vasna: village life in Gujarat
Brian Durrans   53

1 Introduction   55

2 Vasna: the present   57
   *Agriculture 57 Village structure 59 Caste and ritual
   pollution 61 The house 63 Domestic equipment 69
   Food 75 Dress 77 Festivals and fairs 78 Bullock carts 81
   Pot making 82 Weaving 85*

3 Vasna: the past   88
   *The Harappan legacy 88 Production and trade before
   1630 89 Production and trade after 1630 91*

Further reading   94

Index   95

Acknowledgements

Brian Durrans's contribution to this book is based on two brief visits to Gujarat in 1980, concerned with preparing the exhibition 'Vasna: Inside an Indian Village'. The director and staff of the National Institute of Design in Ahmedabad provided efficient help and accommodation. Considerable assistance was obtained from the Gujarat State Handloom and Handicraft Development Corporation. For introductions in the villages and for his unflagging friendship, interest and support thanks are due to Shri Haku Shah, and to his family for their warm hospitality. Shri Sukumar Trivedi undertook the interpreting and other roles with efficiency and good humour. Shri Dahyabhai Chauhan and his fellow villagers and neighbours were extremely helpful. The influence of Dr V. S. Pramar's thesis (see Further reading) is gratefully acknowledged, but he is not responsible for any errors in this book.

Robert Knox is grateful to Dr F. R. Allchin of Cambridge University for permission to use data appearing in his forthcoming joint publication (see Further reading), to Mr B. K. Thapar, former Director-General of the Archaeological Survey of India, Mr W. Zwalf and Mr Joe Cribb of the British Museum and Miss Mena Brient. The staff of several institutions have assisted in the preparation of the exhibition 'From Village to City in Ancient India' connected with the publication of this book. Mr J. P. Joshi, Miss Madhu Bala and Dr B. S. Verma, of the Archaeological Survey of India, Professor G. R. Sharma and Mr D. Mandal, of Allahabad University, Professor S. B. Deo and Dr M. K. Dhavalikar, of the Deccan College, Poona, should also be acknowledged.

The authors are indebted to Dr Kapila Vatsyayan at the Ministry of Education and Culture, New Delhi, to the Indian Advisory Committee of the Festival of India, to the Indian High Commission in London, and to the staff of the British Council, both in New Delhi and Bombay. They are also grateful to the following for their kind permission to reproduce photographs:

Archaeological Survey of India: 20–2, 26–33, 35, 41, 45, 48–50

Department of Ancient History, Culture, and Archaeology, University of Allahabad: 16, 19

Ashmolean Museum, Oxford: 47

Deccan College, Poona: 37–8

India Office Library and Records: 84

Shri Haku Shah: *front cover*, 66, 81, 85

Victoria and Albert Museum (Crown Copyright reserved): 64 (right)

Preface

India is blessed with a cultural heritage which is unsurpassed elsewhere both in richness and variety. The diversity of this great heritage is conditioned largely by geographical and ecological factors which have turned certain parts of the country into areas of attraction and others into areas of isolation or culs-de-sac. While the former show a pattern of developing cultures through the movement of ideas and peoples, the latter exhibit the continuing traditions and technology of primitive societies unaffected by civilising processes. A uniform pattern of cultural development is, therefore, not possible for a country of the size and cultural diversity of India, where Stone Age communities practising a farming economy were living contemporaneously with fully urbanised cultures while still retaining their essential separateness and self-sufficiency. At the same time, although India was subjected to the so-called Urban Revolution – with the rise of the Indus Civilisation in the mid-third millennium BC and again some two millennia later with the emergence of the sixteen *mahajanapadas*, in the sixth century BC – traditional and economic ethos has been characteristically rural.

The exhibitions 'From Village to City in Ancient India' and 'Vasna: Inside an Indian Village' have appropriately been chosen to highlight this recurrent phenomenon in Indian cultural history. The scope of this book, reflecting that of the exhibitions, extends from the Neolithic period, showing farming and animal husbandry in the sixth millennium BC, through the successive urban phases of copper/bronze and iron, to the development of art and architecture and religious institutions and the establishment of universities in the sixth to twelfth centuries AD. A description of life in a modern rural Indian setting follows based upon villages in the Ahmedabad region of Gujarat, so that aspects of both ancient and modern village cultures are neatly juxtaposed in one volume. The archaeological section serves as a general historical background to the later section and emphasises the long process of development that has continued in India since ancient times. On the occasion of the Festival of India (1982) it is a pleasure to introduce a work comprising subjects which, though closely related, are so often dealt with in isolation.

B. K. THAPAR
Former Director-General, Archaeological Survey of India

PART ONE

FROM VILLAGE TO CITY IN ANCIENT INDIA

Robert Knox

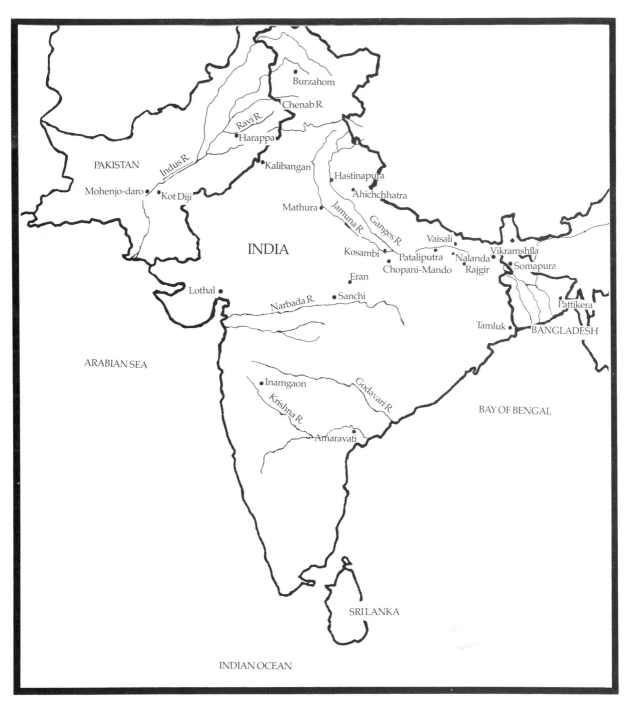

CHAPTER ONE
Introduction

India has a population of more than 600 million people. Something like a sixth, therefore, of all the people on earth come from the Indian subcontinent, and it is the origins of their settled life which will be surveyed in this book. Beginning with the earliest evidence for clusters of houses in the Ganges valley, this development will be traced through the Indus Civilisation to the great urban period in the late centuries BC. Finally, the florid richness of the last great period of Buddhist monastery building in eastern India in about the tenth century AD will be explored.

Sources of information for this very long period are various. For the first few thousand years from pre-Neolithic times to the Iron Age we have to rely almost entirely upon evidence of the spade. It is only through exploration and excavation of ancient sites that anything is known of the life of the most ancient peoples of the subcontinent.

During later periods when the foundations of the great literature of ancient India were laid there are textual sources which tell us a great deal about life in cities and villages. At the same time, however, archaeological data highlights the general picture of settled life provided by the texts, offers concrete evidence for developments often only hinted at, and yields examples of material culture inaccessible on the printed page or from a manuscript. Unlike China or other great ancient cultures, India does not have a tradition of precise historical study: information about everyday life comes usually only incidentally to the statement of religious or philosophical principles and legal or political discussion. The historical facts of ancient India have been gathered together largely through the efforts of scholars who, during the last two centuries, have concentrated on the examination of the physical remains of ancient India. The study of ancient technology, architecture, inscriptions, coinage, town planning and art have led to the painting of a fairly clear background to the great events of the past as they have affected India and her neighbours. In concentrating on a small number of areas and sites to illustrate the various stages that emerge a general impression of the full picture is evoked.

CHAPTER TWO

Rural bias

Entrance to the valley at Rajgir, ancient capital of the kingdom of Magadha, now in the modern state of Bihar. Massive stone fortifications stretch from summit to summit of the hills enclosing the entire vast expanse of the valley.

A modern bullock cart of traditional design, similar in style and construction to types known in ancient India.

A single and vitally important theme to be borne in mind is that settled life in India begins and ends in the villages of the subcontinent; cities are a subsidiary development.

The first settlements in India, and, of course, Pakistan and Bangladesh, were very likely to have been temporary in nature: campsites, stone-tool factory areas, rock shelters, caves, and so on. In due course small clusters of houses emerged in the middle Ganges plains and may be regarded as being fore-runners of the hundreds of thousands of villages in which the overwhelming majority of all the people of South Asia live. Throughout the events of the past 10,000 years the Indian village has endured as the soul of life in the subcontinent. Invaders have come and gone, empires have risen and fallen, periods of city life have flourished and sunk into decline, but the villages have remained. The theme of this book is, therefore, that underlying everything in India is a village continuity. This is as true for the ancient period as it is for the present. It is the cultural backdrop against which every event occurs, simply because the villages have always vastly outnumbered the towns and cities.

Cities

During two periods in ancient India this village continuity was punctuated by the rise of city life. The first of these developments began in the early centuries of the third millennium BC and lasted from that incipient stage through a mature urban period to decline and disappearance by about 2000 BC. This is the period of the Indus Civilisation, based for the most part in the area of the Indus River and its tributaries in Pakistan, but overlapping very considerably into modern political India, the states of Rajasthan and Gujarat in particular.

More than 1,000 years later a second growth of city life began on the great plains of north India, this time in the area of the Ganges River. After 1000 BC small agricultural villages where inhabitants used iron tools grew gradually into massive, walled cities. By roughly the middle of the millennium these great urban centres were the homes of a sophisticated and civilised population, practising the arts, writing, using a variety of coinage, and trading far and wide. That period saw also the rise, along with the cities, of a series of large political units in north India. These *mahajanapadas*, as they were called, were divided into republics and kingdoms. The great cities of the Ganges were the capitals of these states. This second urban period was the time during which the great part of the foundations of modern Indian city life was laid. There is, in the main, a continuity of urban life from that time to the present, despite the unhappy fact that it is largely a history of endless dynastic struggle, invasion and destruction that characterises this long period.

Some of the great cities of the ancient Ganges plains are overlain by modern centres. Pataliputra, capital of the Emperor Ashoka in the third century BC, is the site of modern Patna in the state of Bihar; on the banks of the Ganges at

Benares the site of Rajghat marks the capital of the ancient republic of Kasia. Other great ancient cities such as Rajgir, Ahichchhatra, Sravasti, Hastinapur, Vaisali and Kausambi lie in ruins, their positions marked only by the outline of their collapsed city walls and the scattering of broken pottery that is the hallmark of every ancient mound in the subcontinent. It is important to remember that the urban traditions developed in these now dead cities have endured to the present and that they represent a continuity parallel to that of the ubiquitous Indian village.

CHAPTER THREE

The first settlements

A Mesolithic rock-shelter in Mirzapur District, Uttar Pradesh.

The earliest inhabitants of the Indian subcontinent did not live in villages. Their culture is characterised by the use of stone tools of various types, and these are the basis of what is known about the details of their lives. In the earliest periods of the Indian Paleolithic or Old Stone Age large lumps of stone were fashioned into hand axes and chopping tools. Such tools are known from sites in nearly every part of the country from north to south. Nothing is known of the settlements themselves, although caves, rocky outcrops and temporary shelters were probably the best early man could manage for himself. The Middle Paleolithic of 30,000–50,000 years ago is characterised by the use of tools made from flakes of stone, a considerable refinement over the cobble tools of the earlier stage. Regrettably, we know little more about settlement patterns or the details of Middle Stone Age life than for the preceding period. It is only with the advance of the millennia into the post-Pleistocene era and the gradual refinement and reduction in size of the stone tools used by early man in India that something of the earliest history of settled life in north India begins to unfold.

Recent work in the region of the middle Ganges plains in the valley of the Belan River near Allahabad have yielded evidence of what may be the earliest settlements in India. Although the flood plains of the Ganges are not sources of the raw materials of a stone-tool-using people, the neighbouring Vindhyan Plateau and the stone-rich beds of such rivers as the Belan and its tributaries were ideal for this purpose.

A long sequence of human occupation of this area is discernible from the Lower Paleolithic onwards, and gives evidence of the earliest-known settlement in north India. Adjacent to the rocky Vindhya Hills where early man lived near to his sources of stone the flood plain of the Ganges was characterised by an environment rich in plant and animal life. All over this region the remains of the great river's old courses formed horseshoe lakes, attractive sources of food for early man as the climate of the Vindhyas grew in aridity. The hills and river flowing through them provided raw materials for stone-tool making. Migrations on to the plains by the hunting and gathering people began and, with an easy supply of stone near by, small settlements grew up in the region of these old lakes and river courses.

Chopani-Mando

The site of Chopani-Mando on a terrace of the Belan River near Allahabad is the earliest kind of settlement known in north India. Its stone-tool assemblage is apparently of a type showing a transition from the larger flakes of the Upper Paleolithic to the finer and increasingly smaller and more refined flakes and blades of the Mesolithic or Middle Stone Age. The site was occupied from that earliest period to a time when the characteristic microliths were associated with polished stone tools such as ringstones, grinders and querns. A fragile, hand-made pottery appears as well in the later stages at this site.

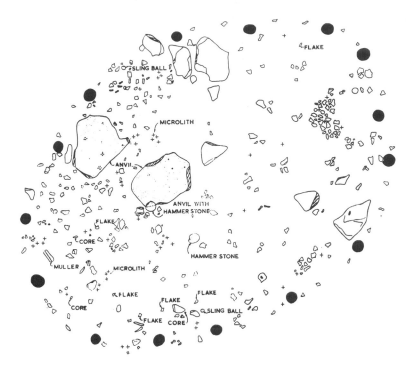

Floor plan of a hut from Chopani-Mando, the earliest-known village site in India, showing the positions of various stone artefacts. The black spots mark the positions of postholes. The hut is about 2·5 m at its longest.

Of special importance at this site was the discovery of a series of hut foundations. The excavators of Chopani-Mando suggest that these semi-permanent structures began to appear in the second or early Mesolithic period. The huts vary from nearly 4 m in diameter at the earliest to almost 5 m by the time the site was abandoned. They are round or oval and are built of upright wooden posts set up to 1 m apart with the intervening spaces walled in with reeds plastered with mud. There is evidence that part of the floor area may have been paved with small stones. On the floors of these huts a predictable deposit of domestic rubbish was found – pieces of waste stone, microliths, fragments of bone, lumps of burnt clay and potsherds.

In the latest stage of the site as many as thirteen of these huts were un-covered, all placed in close proximity to each other. Between the huts small round pits containing ashy soil and domestic waste were found. With a diameter of only 1 m these are probably the remains of rubbish pits. The excavators suggest further the existence of storage bins made of bamboo and clay and floored with flat stone slabs. Within the huts themselves flat stone anvils and hammer-stones along with waste flakes, cores and numerous micro-liths suggest that tool making took place in the individual structures and was not restricted to any particular area of the settlement. There is therefore no craft specialisation evident at this site. The later period of Chopani-Mando yielded cattle and sheep or goat bones along with specimens of wild rice.

The economy of the settlement was essentially that of hunting and gather-ing, and there is no evidence for domestication of either plants or animals, although some incipient agriculture is suggested. The character of the settle-ment at Chopani-Mando is likewise uncertain; the site may have been seasonal or semi-permanent serving the possibly migratory life-style of its inhabitants. The deposit of more than 1·5 m suggests a duration of many centuries. Abso-lute dates derived from deposits bearing a similar material culture suggest a date in the ninth millennium BC for the later period at Chopani-Mando, although the precise chronology of this and related sites has yet to be securely defined.

Mahadaha

Moving down from the Vindhyas to the horseshoe lakes of the Ganges plain, early man found a ready source of both water and abundant wild food. The recently excavated Mesolithic site of Sarai Nahar Rai and Mahadaha (Pratap-garh District), both situated at the edge of lakes, were probably seasonal camping grounds, as the ancient deposits there are often only very shallow. At both these sites, however, the discovery of a number of human graves suggests a pattern of burial practises and occupation of at least a semi-permanent nature. Most of the skeletons were oriented with their heads towards the west. Some of them wore antler ornaments in the form of pendants, necklaces and rings, possibly the earliest such adornments known in the subcontinent. The graves also contained burial goods in the form of bone articles, burnt animal bones, microliths and bone arrowheads. Within the cemetery area hearths were found, although no hut foundations have been uncovered.

Mahadaha was settled again and again, as the disturbance of one burial by another clearly attests. Judging by the vast concentration of wild animal bones uncovered at the site and the strong arrowhead component in the tool assemblage, Mahadaha was a hunting camp occupied and reoccupied. Its inhabitants fished in the lake and gathered wild grains which they processed with stone querns and rubbing-stones.

The first settlements in India are of an expectedly rudimentary kind but are part of a long evolution from the Paleolithic into a later period when stone tools were small, technically very refined and functionally specialised. The social structure or precise economy of settlements such as Chopani-Mando at the edge of the Vindhya Hills or Mahadaha on the plains is not revealed by the material excavated there. These sites and hundreds like them were not the scene of events of great historical importance as were the cities of later millennia; they were, however, a first important link in a chain of development leading up to the complex settlement forms of the future. Even if these were not the precise ancestors of such cities as Kausambi or Sankissa, they represent the idea of groups of people banding together in some way for mutual benefit or convenience, which is fundamental to any settlement, large or small. By a very early date, therefore, evidence is to be found for the principle of settlement in the middle Ganges region and the way paved for future developments associated with an increasingly complex technology and economy.

It is interesting to note that survivals of the Stone Age way of life are to be found in modern India in certain tribal groups, some until recently known to use stone tools and live in shelters not unlike their ancestors in Mesolithic times.

CHAPTER FOUR

Neolithic villages

The Indian Neolithic presents a varied picture and ranges in somewhat differing forms from the Kashmir in the north-west to the south and east of the country. Some of these areas can be only very sketchily described during this stage of development and are defined solely on the basis of types of polished stone axes, settlements being entirely unknown. Neolithic sites in central Uttar Pradesh and in the Vale of Kashmir, however, have yielded important information about the nature of settlements of this period. The earliest Neolithic settlements in the subcontinent are to be found in Baluchistan in Pakistan and date, at least in the case of Mehrgarh in Kachi District, to the seventh millennium BC. Out of a series of developments stemming from that period in western Pakistan came the first urban period in the subcontinent, the Indus Civilisation. The Indian Neolithic is not related to those developments and, by and large, is much later in date than that of Baluchistan. It is, however, in large part the direct ancestor of later copper-using settlements of the post-Indus Civilisation period. The character of settlements in Neolithic India is important as a link in what seems a virtually unbroken evolution from earliest times.

Mahagara

Only three kilometres from Chopani-Mando on the Belan River are the twin sites of Mahagara and Koldihwa, each on opposite banks of the stream. The Neolithic deposits at Koldihwa are known from only a very small excavation of the relevant levels at the site. Handmade pottery and ground-stone implements, stone blades and microliths characterise this period. The remains of rice impressions in potsherds have been identified as a domestic variety. Radiocarbon dates from the deposit suggest dates for this material in the seventh, sixth and fifth millennia, an extremely early chronology awaiting verification.

Mahagara, on the opposite bank of the Belan River, was extensively excavated and yielded much valuable information about settlements of the period. In general terms Neolithic settlements were permanent villages with an agriculture-based economy. Because of the season-to-season, work-intensive nature of the economy these villages are seen to have been inhabited over long periods of time, many centuries in some cases. They are usually situated close to a permanent water supply and with easy access to necessary natural resources. In the case of Mahagara in the hilly tract at the edge of the Ganges plains the locality in ancient times must have been full of wild animals used to supplement the ordinary food-producing economy.

Twenty hut foundations have been uncovered at Mahagara, eighteen belonging to a single constructional phase. These structures were all circular or oval in shape and varied in diameter from about 3 m to nearly 6·5 m. Wooden posts held up the roof, and walls, which were built of reeds, bamboo, grass, etc., were plastered with mud as at Chopani-Mando and at many sites of succeeding periods. Bamboo was a favourite building material, and it is suggested that the roofs were conical.

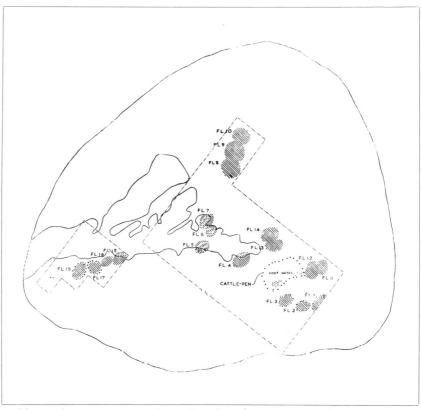

Site plan of Mahagara, a Neolithic village on the Belan River, with clusters of huts and a cattle-pen. The site is about 60 m wide.

Obviously it is not insignificant that these huts are found in clusters of two and three arranged in a rough line with their foundations overlapping. This was not a crowded village as at Chopani-Mando; the house units are well spaced, relative to each other, distances as much as 12 m being recorded between two units.

A much richer material culture is presented to us at Mahagara. The usual deposit of domestic detritus contains large quantities of pottery of wares of several types, including cord-impressed and burnished red, stone blades, microliths, sling balls, querns, rubbing-stones, bone points, burnt animal bones and terracotta beads. Storage jars and vessels for cooking and eating are part of the assemblage.

A fascinating aspect of the economy of the Neolithic people of Mahagara was revealed by the discovery of a cattle-pen at the end of the village nearest to the river bank. The area was surrounded by wooden posts presumably to support fencing of some kind. There were three openings in this fence and, with easy access to water, it was an ideal place for the penning up of a village herd. Hoof impressions of cattle of various age groups were discovered within the area of the pen. Outside it, near the hut clusters, the hoof imprints of sheep or goats were found. Around the cattle-pen four house-unit clusters were placed, presumably for added protection of the animals.

A careful distributional analysis of the artefacts discovered at Mahagara has led to the conclusion that the huts were not simply multi-purpose dwelling and industrial areas: the relative absence of stone tools, wasters, cores, etc. from some huts suggests that they were used for purposes other than the manufacture of stone tools. A corresponding concentration of such material in other huts suggests strongly that a craft specialisation was to some degree present at the site. Each of the house units seems, on the other hand, to have been furnished with a full range of articles necessary for domestic self sufficiency – querns, milling-stones and a range of household vessels.

The division of the village into relatively independent family units seems likely, but the need for communal protection of the herds is clearly demonstrated by the proximity of the cattle-pen to a number of hut clusters. We can assume, no doubt, similar co-operation in other areas of community life, although the archaeological record does not provide any more evidence. The excavators of Mahagara have suggested that the basic economy of the settlement was oriented solely towards subsistence with no emphasis on the production of surpluses. There seems no good reason to doubt this conclusion, but if any evidence were available concerning the extent of cultivation of the flood plain near the site, suggesting how much food could be produced in a season, further comment might be possible. The close proximity of the Neolithic deposit at Koldihwa just across the river suggests some relationship between the two settlements. It might be reasonable to imagine the existence of some small-scale bartering and, probably, social relations of other sorts.

The population of the village at Mahagara has been estimated to be about 150 inhabitants.

Burzahom

A further and relatively isolated area of the Indian Neolithic is seen in a series of sites in the Vale of Kashmir, the principal being the well-known village at Burzahom. The settlement at this site is in no way similar to the complex of hut clusters and cattle-pen at Mahagara. It differs also in that it is related only to

General view of the excavations at Burzahom in the Kashmir.

A partially excavated pit house at Burzahom.

sites in northern Pakistan and may even have some connection with Neolithic complexes in East Asia. The climate of the region around Burzahom is much more severe than in the Ganges plain or the Vindhyas. The coldness of the Kashmiri winter obliged the people of Burzahom to devise a system of shelter which would protect them from these extremes of climate.

The neolithic at Burzahom is characterised by a unique complex of pit houses. Some of these were excavated on a very large scale and area of two general types, circular and square. In the first period as many as sixteen of these subterranean dwellings were discovered cut directly into the hard loess-type soil of the area. The largest of these pits were almost 4 m in depth, its circular opening nearly 3 m in diameter, with the living area at the bottom of the pit at the earliest stage widening to a diameter of over 4·5 m. Three landing steps at the opening to this large pit suggest the use of a ladder of some sort for gaining entrance to the living area. The discovery of a series of post holes around the entrance suggests the existence of a kind of superstructure erected to protect the inhabitants of the pit house from the elements. Near the mouths

21

of the pits a number of hearths of the same period were found, along with a series of shallow storage pits.

When weather permitted, the pit dwellers of Neolithic Burzahom could live in the open. Pit houses are excellent protection also against the heat of summer and year-round occupation cannot be ruled out. The floors of the pits were flat and the interior walls were sometimes plastered. Gradually the dwellings at Burzahom began to fill up with domestic rubbish, and the deposits unearthed in them contained large quantities of ash and charcoal. Fires for cooking and warmth were probably lit inside the pits, and when the pits became too full to be used as houses, they may well have been used as rubbish dumps.

The second period at Burzahom is also a Neolithic deposit, but the pit houses had been abandoned by that time, filled to the brim with domestic detritus. Some of the pit openings appear to have been plastered with mud and red ochre to form a living floor. The discovery of complexes of post holes in association with these floors suggests that the inhabitants of Burzahom had abandoned their ancestral pits in favour of shelter above ground. The precise character of these later structures is not known.

The material culture and burial practises of the people of Burzahom are equally unique and interesting. The tool assemblage from the site is made of stone, bone and antler. Ground-stone axes, ringstones, adzes, points, drills, querns and rubbing-stones and other types form the stone collection. An

A series of above-ground features from Neolithic Burzahom, including the foundations of a rectangular structure.

attractive greenish-blue in colour, the stone has a fine grain and lends itself well to refined work. There was no stone-blade industry at Burzahom in distinct contrast to Mahagara. Coarse grey and black burnished pottery with mat impressions on their bases are typical of this complex, as are a wide variety of bone points, needles, awls and harpoons.

The most characteristic stone-tool shape from Burzahom is the rectangular 'harvester' knife perforated with two holes at one edge. Found also in bone at Burzahom, this harvester knife is virtually identical with similar objects found in Neolithic China – a parallel which has led to much speculation as to the origin of the Burzahom Neolithic. The harvester and a number of animal burials suggest some evidence for a link between the Kashmir and East or Central Asia, although at this stage the precise mechanism of such a connection cannot be defined.

The discovery of a number of animal burials, especially of wild dogs arranged in what would appear to have been some definite ritual fashion, suggests something about the ideology of the period. Wolf and ibex burials, as well as animal bones or complete animal skeletons, were also found buried in graves with human remains. Little or no grave-goods were placed in the human graves, although sometimes red ochre was applied to the bones in the case of secondary interments.

The absence of querns for the grinding of grains seems to suggest that the economy of the villagers at Burzahom was based more or less exclusively on hunting. An incised stone panel bearing what is plainly a hunting scene depicts a stag being attacked by two hunters, one with a lance and the other drawing a bow. Also shown is a dog, possibly a domestic variety which was used in the hunt.

A human burial from Burzahom. In this grave are the skeletons of an adult and child.

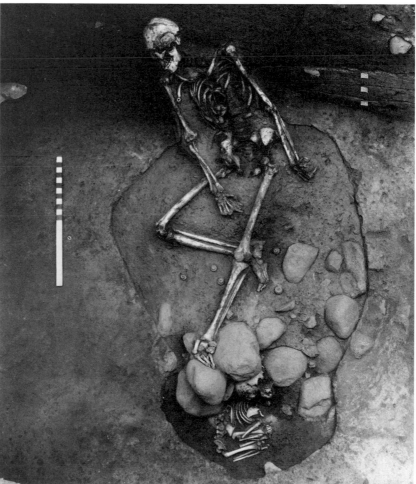

CHAPTER FIVE

Village to city

The earliest settlements in the Indian subcontinent are found far to the west in Pakistani Baluchistan where a tradition of village building began between 7,000 and 8,000 years ago. This stage is first seen in the first Neolithic levels at the vast ancient site of Mehrgarh in Sibi District, a period characterised by the presence of ground-stone tools and no pottery. The sequence at Mehrgarh, after several recent seasons' excavations by a team of French scholars, can be seen now to provide a continuous and unbroken occupation from the eighth millennium BC and its aceramic Neolithic to a period contemporary with the mature Indus Civilisation in the middle of the third millennium BC. We can see in this something of the long process of local evolution that eventually led to the foundation of the great Indus culture area with its major urban centres in the Sind and Rajasthan. The geographical focus of the Indus Civilisation was principally in what is modern Pakistan, although the overlap into modern India is very extensive. Sites of the period are numerous in north-west India, Rajasthan and Gujarat.

One of the three known large city sites of the Indus culture is at Kalibangan in western Rajasthan. The importance of this vast early civilisation in the history of settlements in the Indian subcontinent cannot be over-emphasised. It is the first of the two great urban periods known in India and, although it fell into decline and eventually disappeared, its influence can still be felt in traditional Indian culture today. Certainly it shares with modern India many similar traits, from certain aspects of religion to weights and measures and even the generalities of house plans. Although it is known primarily from the excavation of the large city sites, Harappa, Mohenjo-daro and Kalibangan, the Indus Civilisation was a complex of cities and villages, the latter growing up first out of the aceramic Neolithic of the early period and as a category of settlement enduring long beyond the end of the first urbanisation. From the name of the Indus Civilisation-type site, Harappa, the term 'Harappan' is derived. It is used virtually interchangeably with 'Indus Civilisation'.

Before continuing with a description of Indus towns and villages some general remarks should be made about the chronology and spread of settlements in the subcontinent. Between about 7000 and 8000 BC and 5000 BC a Neolithic culture developed in Baluchistan based on the use of stone tools, polished tools, blades and microliths. Pottery was known, though not at first, and settlements took the form of small permanent villages. The precise beginnings of this culture are not known, as even in the aceramic Neolithic stage at Mehrgarh the settlement was already composed of permanent houses made of mud brick and organised along regular lines. The settlement stage preceding the first period at Mehrgarh has yet to be discovered. Between 5000 and 3500 BC the growth of copper-using, or Chalcolithic, cultures in Baluchistan took place. This was a development limited to the western part of the subcontinent, Baluchistan in particular.

After about 3500 BC at least two processes can be seen to have begun in varying parts of the Indo-Pakistan area. First, settlements began to spread into the Indus system, from Baluchistan into the Sind, Punjab and eastern extensions of the system. Between about 3000 and 3500 BC the growth of the precise antecedents of the Indus Civilisation took place, the pre- or early Indus period as it is sometimes called. During this time the formation of large complex settlements was achieved. True urbanisation did not have to wait for the overwhelming cultural rigidity of the mature Indus period. Great sites such as Rahman Dheri and Gumla in the North-west Frontier Province, Kot Diji near Khairpur, and Tarakai Qila in Waziristan all give evidence of large size, planning and monumental architecture, often including massive city walls. By about the second half of the fourth millennium BC most of these characteristics had become established in what became the Indus Civilisation culture area.

Simultaneously, settlements began to appear beyond the Indus. The first Neolithic settlements in north India, at Mahagara and Burzahom, have already been described in some detail. The precise chronology of these sites is still some way from being established. Current thinking places them in the period following 3500 BC, during the time when urban forms were beginning to emerge in the Indus flood plains. The earliest cities in India are, therefore, a product of developments that began in Baluchistan and the Indus area. The Neolithic villages of north India bear no direct relation to the early Indus cities and villages with which, for the most part, they are contemporary. The descendants of these Indian Neolithic settlements are later north Indian and Peninsular Chalcolithic and Iron Age villages, some of which ultimately grew into the great cities of the Ganges plains in the last millennium BC.

The Indus Civilisation

At the height of its maturity the Indus Civilisation dominated for some 500 years between 2500 and 2000 BC a vast area encompassing nearly all of modern Pakistan, stretching east to beyond modern Delhi, to the south into Saurashtra and to the west along the Makran coast of Baluchistan, and was known even as far distant as a small site in northern Afghanistan. The backbone of this culture system was the Indus River and its numerous tributaries. Sites of the period, large and small, are found usually near the banks of these rivers, and the greatest site of them all, Mohenjo-daro, lies close to the Indus itself. The flood plains on which these settlements were located provided a rich foundation for the basic agricultural economy of the mass of the people. The rivers provided the means whereby a culture of such undoubted organic strength could grow and flourish. The arteries along which trade, commerce and communication took place, these rivers linked the great cities of the Indus with the open seas and aided contact with states in other parts of the ancient world, Mesopotamia in particular. The Indus Civilisation resembles the other great ancient cultures, China, Egypt and Mesopotamia, in that it grew up on the broad flood plains of a vast and dominating river. Unlike the ancient civilisations of China and Egypt, the Harappan culture fell into decline and disappeared with hardly a trace. It was only through excavations beginning in the 1920s that the cities and villages of the Indus began to emerge after nearly 4,000 years of obscurity.

The chief characteristic of the Indus Civilisation is not simply that the area occupied by it was so enormous but that throughout that area a rigid similarity was maintained in nearly every aspect of its culture. Sites of the Harappan period are instantly recognisable as certain typical features are to some extent always present. The black-decorated red pottery, with typical fish-scale or pipal-leaf patterns, steatite seals, terracotta cakes, perforated pottery, both mud and baked brick construction, terracotta figurines and so on are all characteristic of the material culture of Indus sites. The reasons for this uniformity are not known. It is impossible to say at this stage precisely why the various urbanised cultures of pre-Indus Baluchistan and the Sind were more or less suddenly transformed into such a regularly arranged complex of basic traits. What must be clear, however, is that this uniformity was defined and administered in some way, since it is known that the culture lasted for some 500 years and changed little in basic character in all that time. Some mechanism must have been present which provided a stable, convincing and probably highly disciplined influence in the face of which uniformity was maintained with only slight provincial variation. If the decline and fall of the Indus Civilisation is to be sought anywhere, it ought to be in discovering precisely how this socio-economic, cultural or political authority was undermined and why, towards the end of the Indus era, a decline in urban standards became apparent with subsequent abandonment of the cities.

Town planning

There were at least three great cities of the Indus Civilisation. The first of these was Harappa in Sahiwal District of the Punjab in Pakistan, discovered in the last century by General Cunningham, of the Archaeological Survey of India. It lies near an old bed of the Ravi River, a tributary of the Indus. The second, and

General view of the ancient mounds marking the site of Kalibangan, which with Harappa and Mohenjo-daro is the third great city of the Indus Civilisation.

most extensively excavated of all the Indus sites, is Mohenjo-daro on the right bank of the Indus in the Sind. The third of these Indus 'capitals' is Kalibangan in Ganganagar District, Rajasthan, and the only major city of the period on Indian soil. This site was excavated with modern archaeological accuracy in the early 1960s and has yielded a vast quantity of new data highlighting the previously somewhat limited picture of life in Indus times.

Each of these three great cities was arranged in similar fashion. The streets of the Harappan cities were often laid out with mathematical accuracy, uniform widths and a system of city blocks being the principle of the arrangement. The alignments were not rigid in pattern, especially at Mohenjo-daro, but, generally speaking, the idea of town planning was well established in these cities, although they were never carbon copies of each other. Town planning as described here did not regulate life to that extent, but it certainly and obviously dictated the general principles of town and street alignment and size, the existence of communal drains and refuse pits, and, probably, communal food storage. The end result of this sort of planning was not a settlement uniform in every detail but one that was organised along sensibly predictable lines to the apparent convenience of its inhabitants.

Typically, the form taken by these major centres consists of two areas of occupation. A large, probably residential area is complemented by a smaller 'citadel' to the west, built on a platform of mud brick. Both of these parts of the city are surrounded by heavy walls of baked and mud brick. The main streets seem to run uniformly from north to south. At Kalibangan the early Indus town consisted of only a single walled rectangle, but by 2500 BC the typical citadel and lower town of the Indus city had been constructed. We can only guess at the precise function of these citadels, but there seems little doubt that they served as some kind of administrative centre. No one knows how the

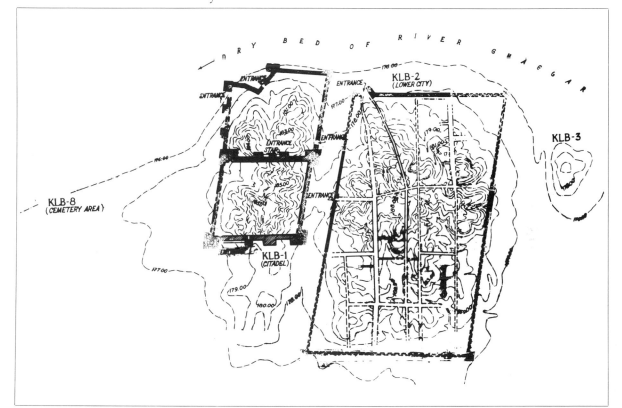

Plan of the Harappan city at Kalibangan, showing the citadel to the upper left and the lower town to the right. From north to south the site is about 400 m in length.

people of the Indus were governed, whether there were kings, emperors, priest kings, tyrants or oligarchies. None of the excavations at any of the major sites has been able to contribute significantly to answering that question, least of all the citadel mounds. It is clear, however, from what is known of these citadels that they contained buildings of monumental character usually placed on large brick platforms and protected by heavy fortification. The most famous structure of any in the Indus region is the Great Bath at Mohenjo-daro. It is situated in a prominent position at the summit of the citadel there and probably served some ritual ablutive purpose now long forgotten. Along with this structure buildings described as 'granary', 'assembly hall', and 'college' were

An excavated area of the citadel mound at Kalibangan showing a cluster in the foreground of what have been interpreted as fire altars. A brick-lined drain runs in a curve across the platform bearing the altars.

uncovered. With the exception of the Great Bath these identifications are largely fanciful and contribute little to our understanding of the precise role of the citadel in the life of the Indus city.

The citadel at Kalibangan was more carefully excavated, and the data recovered there rather more accurately characterise its plan. The citadel was rectangular in shape and was divided into two parts by a transverse wall. The northern half contained what appear to be residential buildings with no trace, apparently, of the monumental structures uncovered at Mohenjo-daro. The southern half yielded a complex of massive mud-brick platforms, possibly as many as six in all. These platforms were not joined to the fortifications and were separated from each other by passages of varying width. Only sparse traces of the buildings that once stood on them were found. Two of the platforms, however, yielded evidence of what seem unmistakably to be ritual practices. On one platform a large rectangular cistern made of burnt brick was found to contain a collection of cattle bones and deer antlers, possibly some kind of sacrifice. On another of these platforms a series of what have been called 'fire altars' was discovered. These take the form of a shallow oval or rectangular pit, containing charcoal and ash, in the centre of which was placed a cylindrical block of clay surrounded by a collection of flat terracotta cakes, either round or triangular in shape.

Closely associated with this complex of altars are an unusually large number of wells and drains suggestive of an important role for water in any ritual practice performed in the citadel at Kalibangan, a phenomenon shown also in the Great Bath at Mohenjo-daro. Significantly, individual fire altars of the type found in the citadel were uncovered in many of the houses of the lower city and, outside the walls of the city, a small group of five such altars were found surrounded by a mud-brick wall. The absence of a significant quantity of occupation debris in the platform area of the citadel at Kalibangan suggests further its probable ritual function. None the less, whether the city as a whole was administered from this citadel or whether it was simply a place of worship for the population of the main part of the complex is still unknown.

The monumentality of the structures at Mohenjo-daro on the other hand argues very forcibly for the citadel there being a kind of administrative head-quarters, probably casting its net much further afield and over a much greater area than just the city. Nothing is known of the nature of the relationship that may have existed between these large cities. They may each have been capitals of provinces or subdivisions of the Indus region; conversely, they may have existed as independent city states. We have no idea of the precise administrative structure of the Indus culture, however.

The people of the Indus Civilisation lived in both cities and villages. Very few details of life in the villages are known since archaeological interest has been focused for the most part on the major sites. As exploration has been extended over the past few decades, however, it has been realised that a large number of small settlements existed and that the human population of the Indus area, much increased since pre-Harappan times, could not have been restricted just to the cities. None of the other known sites of the mature Indus period approaches the three largest in size, nor does any of them give evidence of the presence of a citadel. At best they can be called towns, but more reasonably they are villages. These small settlements are the background against which the greatness of the Harappan culture was displayed and are a vital part of the village continuity that is a main theme of this book.

The lower towns of the three great cities contained the houses of the people, workshops, market-places and, probably, temples. The houses range from elaborate structures with many rooms built around a courtyard to rows of cell-like tenements probably meant for the poorer classes. Characteristic of these houses are the sanitary arrangements built into them. Each multi-roomed dwelling contains a bathroom consisting of a cubicle often with a tiled floor and a system of drains for the release of water: these flowed into communal drains in the streets where they were often covered with bricks or slabs of stone. It has been remarked that privies and drains of the kind discovered in Harappan cities were built in the same way in the cities of the later urban period and they can be found also in villages and towns of north India and Pakistan. Any visitor to a site like Mohenjo-daro is struck by the fact that the survival of drains, soakage pits and bathrooms is one of the principal characteristics of the city. In the absence of so much other information about the life of the Harappans one is wrongly tempted to attach a kind of sewage obsession to the Indus Civilisation, when in reality these features can have been much in the minds of only a few city officials and, of course, the people who cleaned the streets.

Harappan houses had flat roofs, as do all houses of traditional design in modern north India and Pakistan. In the unbearable heat of summer these areas are used for sleeping, undoubtedly a practice in ancient times as well. The houses were often of more than one storey and their walls massive. The impression is that these buildings and the streets along which they were laid out cannot have been very different from towns in the Indus region. The outside walls of the houses present a flat monotonous plane broken only by small entrances to the courtyards within. The streets and lanes are often narrow and crowded with traffic of all kinds, from pedestrians to bullock carts, hawkers, beggars, street traders and stray animals.

A complex of rooms at Kalibangan with tiled floors elaborately decorated with intersecting circles, possible for use as bathing areas.

A street in Kalibangan showing the monotonously regular outside walls of houses. A small lane runs off to the right in front of the man with the pick.

Technology

It is by the uniform technology of the Indus Civilisation that settlements of the period are so easily recognised. The Harappans were copper-using people and manufactured both weapons and attractive vessels of several types. The most famous of all Harappan objects is the dancing-girl figurine from Mohenjo-daro, also made of copper. The principal medium for tool making, however, was stone. Long, very fine, parallel-sided blades were struck from prepared cores of buff chert. From this stone brick-shaped lumps were fashioned and used as drain covers in the streets. Steatite was cut into small blocks and carved into the distinctive inscribed seals of the Harappans. Limestone and alabaster were known, although their use seems restricted to small sculpture. Carnelian beads of varying shapes were made. Most distinctive of all, long and very beautiful barrel-shaped beads, characteristic of the Indus people, show a very high degree of technical skill. Elaborate strings of these long beads were used for personal adornment along with beads of shell, faience and gold. Other ornaments of gold were worn, including fillets for the hair. Conch shell was shaped into spoons, inlay shapes and bangles, the latter of a type made to the present day in India and Pakistan.

Pottery and terracotta are the most widespread material remains of the Indus period. A wide range of shapes was known during the mature period, the most characteristic of them being the dish on stand, cylindrical perforated jars and tall elegant vases with an s-shaped section. The pottery of the Harappans is fine and well fired, and is plain or often decorated in black on a background of red. This painted decoration frequently consists of natural themes, fish scales and stylised flora being among the most popular.

Economy

The Harappan economy probably consisted of at least two sectors, one a subsistence agriculture and the other the production of certain goods or surpluses for trade. Farming was based on the production of grains: two varieties of wheat (*Triticum compactum* or *Triticum sphaerococcum*) are still grown by modern farmers in the region. Barley (*Hordeum vulgare*) was grown as well. Peas,

An ancient ploughed field discovered at Kalibangan showing the practice of cross furrowing which is still known in the area.

The dockyard at the Harappan port of Lothal, 219 by 37 m in area. Along one side is a massive brick wharf, and at one end a spillway helped to control the level of water in the basin.

pulses, melons, sesamum and dates have been found in Harappan sites. Cotton is also known from an isolated find at Mohenjo-daro. At Kalibangan a unique archaeological discovery was made: a ploughed field of the early Indus period was excavated revealing a pattern of cross furrowing, a style of ploughing continued to this day in the area of the site. One crop is grown in a set of furrows running in one direction, and another crop is sown in the furrows running the opposite way.

Important to the farming economy of these early times were humped cattle and buffalo, as well as sheep and goats. A wide range of other domestic and wild animals was known to the Harappans. The production of goods or raw materials for trade is known from early Indus times. At the early Indus stone-tool factory site of Lewan in north-west Pakistan a seal impression of a type known from the early city of Rahman Dheri nearly 160 kilometres away suggests a commerce between the two sites. Such local trade can have only increased in succeeding centuries. The buff-coloured chert used by the Harappans for making their characteristic long stone blades all comes from the Rohri Hills near Sukkur on the Indus. It can be inferred that as wide a trade in chert in its raw or semi-prepared state was actively pursued, since the material is found all over the Indus system in its finished form.

Trade with countries outside the Indus system is likewise undoubted. Contemporary written records from Mesopotamia mention journeys to a place known as Meluhha, usually interpreted to mean the Indian subcontinent. A seal with an engraving of a boat, large enough probably in real life to navigate

32

the rivers and the sea coast, suggests that the Indus people may have ventured out on their own as well. Attached to the small port town of Lothal in Gujarat is a long rectangular brick-lined tank with sluice gates at one end. This structure is interpreted to have been a dockyard into which ships were hauled from the now silted-up river near by for purposes of easy loading and unloading. The bun-shaped ingot of copper found at Lothal suggests contact with smelting sites in the Oman.

Writing

A large corpus of seals bearing short inscriptions is known from the Indus Civilisation. The script in which these inscriptions are written has yet to be deciphered, although it is known that it is read from right to left. A hypothesis that the language of the Harappans might have been Dravidian and, therefore,

Kalibangan, a well lined with wedge-shaped burnt brick.

allied to those of south India has been proposed and is currently being investigated. The decipherment of these seal inscriptions will be of importance in the identification of the language of the Harappans but in their brevity may not reveal very much about the people themselves. Any longer written works that they may have possessed were probably on perishable material and are now lost. Individual ideograms of this script are found inscribed on sherds in early Indus deposits suggesting the local development of the system.

Weights

The Harappans used a standard system of weights made of stone and usually cube-shaped. The system is binary with the traditional Indian ratio 16 (16 annas = 1 rupee) as the probable unit, equivalent to 13·625 g. In an economy relying as it must have done on trade, both internally and abroad, an accurate and uniform system of weights was essential.

Religion

The religion of the Indus Civilisation appears to have been at once complex and in certain general aspects related to traditions as characteristic of modern Hinduism as any ancient system. The presence of large numbers of terracotta mother goddesses and stone representations of phalluses (lingams in modern India) point to a kind of fertility worship. Certain motifs on the Indus seals suggest the origin of the Hindu god Siva in his role as lord of animals; others indicate tree, animal and water worship. The use of water in ritual has already been mentioned in the context of the citadel mounds at Kalibangan and Mohenjo-daro. The dead were buried individually in cemeteries in Indus and early Indus times. Their graves vary in style and often contain quantities of grave-goods in the form of pottery and other materials.

Decline

The Indus Civilisation as a city-based culture experienced a decline towards the end of the third millennium BC culminating in the total loss of the cities as a form of settlement. The uniform standards of town planning so characteristic of the mature period are noticeably absent at the end. Various reasons have been put forward to account for the end of the Indus Civilisation, not the least of which concerns climatic change, the flooding and silting up of the Indus itself; alternatively, violent invasions of Indo-European-speaking people may have put an end to the Indus people and their culture.

Small village sites like Bhagwanpura, Manda and Dadheri in the Indian Punjab now suggest that a continuity existed between what are clearly late Indus levels and later deposits containing grey pottery and the famous Painted Grey Ware of the early Iron Age of the upper Ganges region. Although the word 'overlap' is used by the excavators of these sites when referring to the relationships between the later grey wares and the late Indus material, the existence of a continuity from one to the other can easily be suggested. We are not dealing with two separate populations in these small settlements but probably a single people who have changed their style of pottery. The continuation of the Indus villages beyond the time of the cities indicates that what was lost by the end of the third millennium BC was the structure of administration and cohesion that kept the cities intact. With this system the overall uniformity of Indus material culture and the cities were lost but not all the small villages. The end of the cities should be sought in the mechanism responsible for the breakdown of the administrative organism of the civilisation. What has been transmitted of Indus culture into later times was achieved probably by means of the continued existence of the villages themselves, the culmination of a settlement tradition of great antiquity.

CHAPTER SIX

Return to the villages

With the decline of the great cities and large towns of the mature Indus Civilisation at about the turn of the third and second millennia BC settled life in India returned to its previous exclusively rural bias. In this section two sorts of villages from different parts of the subcontinent will be explored: the first will be those small settlements from the Punjab which provide a vitally important link between the Indus Civilisation and the later cultures of north India; moving to the central plateau of India, the Deccan, the ancient settlement of Inamgaon provides a view of villages geographically distant from the Indus culture area.

Bhagwanpura

Bhagwanpura and Dadheri, both in the Indian Punjab, and Manda on the Chenab River near Jammu are recently excavated village sites which are important in that they show a kind of continuity from the Indus Civilisation through to later periods. Also for the first time they reveal something of the broad outlines of house plans of the period. At Bhagwanpura a late Harappan deposit is seen to merge into levels bearing plain grey pottery and then the fine Painted Grey Ware of the late second millennium BC. The site was placed near the banks of the Saraswati River, and in the first period of occupation solid mud platforms were built, probably to protect the living area against floods.

The large, thirteen-roomed house excavated at Bhagwanpura in the Punjab. With a number of others this site represents a transition from the Indus Civilisation to later periods.

The first habitation remains discernible at this site are a collection of roughly circular huts probably of wattle and daub and having thatched roofs. Both Late Harappan and grey pottery is found in this first-phase settlement. Subsequent to this construction a large, thirteen-roomed house with walls of solid mud was built. There is a corridor separating the two halves of the house and a courtyard open on one side. The grey and Painted Grey pottery of the later periods is found in this structure along with a small proportion of late Harappan remains. Significant in this pottery assemblage are a number of late Harappan ceramic shapes which have been copied in the later grey ware. Bowls, basins, jars and the typical Harappan dish-on-stand are all found in grey pottery at this site. The evidence of this pottery seems to supply a convincing argument for continuous development from one phase to the next.

This house was probably of one storey, had a flat roof and does not differ in any real way from the kinds of houses found in villages in north India today. It is a large and rather impressive structure and was probably the home of a large family unit, as such a dwelling would be in a modern Indian village. A tradition of village housing that has continued to the present day is apparent in this house. Even the building materials have hardly changed over the centuries, although the use of burnt brick grew more common in later times. As far as its foundations are an indication of its upper structure, the Bhagwanpura house is made not of baked or mud brick but of compact mud. Small finds from Bhagwanpura include terracotta figurines, ivory and bone needles, glass bangle fragments, beads and a small bull-shaped pendant in carnelian.

At Dadheri the settlement consisted of huts and solid mud-walled houses built on platforms of rammed mud. The mud-walled houses were found during the period of the movement away from late Harappan wares to the later grey ceramic types. At Manda early Indus pottery, including what appears to be a type first identified at Kot Diji in the Sind, underlays the mature Indus period and merges into it. Subsequently, the late Harappan grows into the grey ware periods of the succeeding stage. The excavators suggest that stone rubble may have been used for building purposes at this site in the early periods.

One of the effects of the discovery of what seems to be a cultural continuity running from the early Indus period at Manda through to the Painted Grey Ware of the late second millennium BC is to question the old suggestion that this grey ceramic is associated with the movement eastwards of Indo-European-speaking people, the Aryans. The movement of these people, associated at first with the apparently semi-nomadic and then farming tribes of the Rigveda, the most ancient of all Indian religious texts, took place some time before 1000 BC. It ended in the establishment of Indo-European languages in north India and of the pantheistic religion of the Aryans with its emphasis on ritual and sacrifice. The Veda mentions the existence of an indigenous people with whom the Aryans were in conflict. This native population may have inhabited the towns and villages of the late Indus period. The Aryans may even have had a hand in the destruction of some of the large settlements at a time when the cities had declined and were at their weakest. For all this theorising, however, the precise archaeological identification of the Vedic Aryans has still not been achieved.

Inamgaon

Far to the south of the Indus plains and those of the Ganges, on the great Deccan plateau, is the Chalcolithic village site of Inamgaon on a bank of the Ghod River in Pune District. Settled first by about 1600 BC, the village lasted until about 700 BC. Three periods are recognised at this site and are associated with variations on a basic theme of black-decorated red pottery, known as Malwa and Jorwe wares. The total area of the remains at Inamgaon is in the

A modern pit house near the ancient site at Inamgaon. Pit houses are known from the earliest level of occupation at the site.

The ancient Chalcolithic village site at Inamgaon on the Ghod River, Pune District, Maharashtra.

region of twenty hectares and gives evidence of the existence of three major settlement stages, the Malwa and the early and late Jorwe periods. The village was placed near to both a good supply of water and the famous and very fertile black cotton soil of the region, where grains such as wheat, barley, rice and, possibly, sorghum were cultivated. The population of Inamgaon lived, in the first or Malwa period, in large rectangular houses irregularly placed in relation to one another. Dwelling pits were discovered as well near the ordinary houses of the time but they disappeared by the next period. The settlement of the early Jorwe period was very large and was characterised by both rectangular and circular houses. Within these regularly aligned dwellings are found *chulahs*, or small ovens, and small platforms for what may have been storage bins and small, lime-plastered pits for the storage of grain.

Whereas the early Jorwe settlement was composed of large rectangular huts arranged more or less in linear fashion, the succeeding late Jorwe stage settlement is quite different. From about 1000 BC for 300 years or so the village at Inamgaon was a cluster of small round huts tightly placed with hardly a metre between each of them. The walls were made of bamboo plastered with mud and cow-dung, and in each house were four flat stones upon which was a four-legged storage jar. A large embankment was erected in the early Jorwe period, probably as a method of flood protection. It was built of undressed stones set in mud. Some evidence for craft specialisation emerges from this site based upon the character of artefacts found in the various dwelling units of the three periods. One large house of the second period consisted of five rooms including a kitchen and a store-room. This impressive structure was located close to a curious building made up of two square rooms containing platforms, pit silos and storage bins. In one half of this structure two large fire pits were found which may have been for communal cooking, as they are today, or for some unknown purpose. This curious feature is identified as either a granary or a shrine, or both.

Burials at Inamgaon were always made beneath house floors. Bodies were placed in legged urns or in a pair of urns with their openings juxtaposed. A large potter's kiln was discovered in both of the Jorwe periods. The later one is like a large clay trough embedded in the ground and resting on a stone foundation. The use of oval cushions of clay with a centre hole and grooved sides upon which pots for firing were put is a unique arrangement.

Beads of various stones were made. Copper was smelted and made into

37

Plan of the early Jorwe settlement at Inamgaon showing a complex of large rectangular houses. The village is about 36m wide.

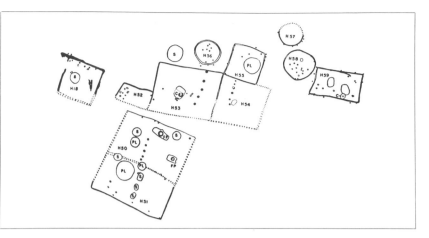

Plan of the late Jorwe settlement at Inamgaon showing the abandonment of the earlier rectangular houses in favour of clusters of round huts. The village is about 30m at its widest.

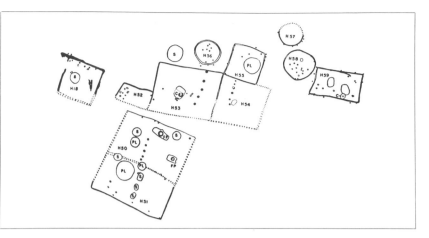

A human burial in a legged urn from Inamgaon, c. 1000 BC.

small ornaments and such things as fish-hooks and other small objects. Gold beads were found along with the smith's crucible and copper tongs. Polished stone axes were also part of the tool assemblage. The religion of the people of Inamgaon is only hinted at in the evidence from the excavation. One interesting object, probably of some religious character, is a headless female figurine found in a clay receptacle with a bull for a mount.

Direct evidence is lacking at Inamgaon for a continuity from the copper- and stone-using stage of settlement life to the Iron Age. At this point, therefore, it would be unwise to infer a distinct relationship between the crowded cluster of small huts that was late Jorwe Inamgaon and later settlements in the Deccan. Such a discovery may yet be made, as certainly it has in regions near by. This deficiency does not alter the fact that in broad outline the villages at Inamgaon do not present a picture altogether different from similar settlements of the subsequent 3,500 years. Small agricultural centres growing a limited number of crops, keeping the usual cattle, sheep and goats, they contain small houses, and with some evidence of craft specialisation associated with kilns and other concentrations of artefacts are a typical phenomenon of even modern India. The details may change: house shape, burial practice, religion, tool types and so on, but the essential way of life has endured regardless of history. This is likewise true of the villages of the Punjab and Kashmir. Some of the details of life may alter over the millennia, a great many may be preserved as well; but the Indian village style of life which began in the Mesolithic period is more or less still with us in the 1980s.

CHAPTER SEVEN

Iron Age and early cities

It was remarked earlier that a continuity can be detected running from the late Harappan in the Punjab through to the Painted Grey Ware period of what became the Iron Age in north India. This continuity and part of the Iron Age of the northern subcontinent can be used to illustrate the origins of the second great flowering of cities in India. In speaking of a continuity it should not be assumed that every single variety of ancient cultural remains in the Ganges, older than any other, is necessarily its direct ancestor. The threads are tangled and, more often, the explanations for certain phenomena and the relationships between others are complex in the extreme. Outside influences bear upon local phenomena and affect them in many ways. These outside forces are influenced, in their turn, by local customs. The end result of such a tangled scheme of development is a complex and rich product. In the Indian context the height of this cultural growth in the ancient world is found in the magnificent cities of the Ganges plains. The influence of these centres spread far and wide in a myriad of ways, but its origins must be seen, despite the twists and turns of the archaeological sequence, in the simple villages of the Gangetic Iron Age and in the relationship of those settlements to more ancient cultural complexes.

The north Indian Iron Age is best known for a number of types of pottery. In the Ganges plains two of the most famous during the pre-urban period are black and red ware, found largely in the middle and lower Ganges area, and Painted Grey Ware. The former often precedes the latter at some intermediate sites from the upper region, but both are contemporary in immediately pre-urban times. Painted Grey Ware, or PGW as it is often called, is typical of the upper reaches of the Ganges and the *doab* or land between the Ganges and the Jamuna. For simplicity's sake examples only of sites containing PGW will be described. The idea of continuity from this earlier period to the later cities need not be repeated for every part of the country.

Small villages of agricultural people are found under nearly every major excavated city site of the middle and late centuries of the last millennium BC. These small settlements differ radically from their cousins in preceding periods in that iron tools had been introduced and that a stone-blade industry played no part in the technology of the time. Villages consisted of groups of huts made of mud-plastered reeds and bamboo on a wooden frame. As in most early sites, lumps of burnt clay bearing the impressions of these building materials are found widely in Iron Age settlements. At the huge mound of Atranjikhera on the Ganges the PGW site uncovered under the massive remains of the later city was found to have an embankment or *bund* around it, the direct ancestor of the city walls of the later complex.

Copper and glass are known at this period, as are objects of terracotta and bone or ivory arrow points. The pottery is wheel-thrown and is most often of a plain red variety. The ceramic assemblage is typified, however, by the PGW mentioned earlier – a fine, thin-walled, grey ware bearing geometric patterns painted in black. Dots, lines and circles in various combinations are typical of the decoration. The commonest forms taken by this Painted Grey Ware are the so-called tray-bowl and cup. The former is usually a flat low-sided bowl resembling to a great degree the *thali* or flat food dish of the modern Indian. The cup or bowl is smaller and has higher sides; it was probably used for drinking, together with the tray-bowl.

Evidence for cultivation of food grains at this period is scanty. Rice is known at Hastinapur and Noh, but no wheat has been found. The bones of humped cattle, buffalo, sheep, goat and pigs are well known at this time. The bones of deer, fish and horses have also been recovered, pointing to a mixed diet of domestic and wild meat. Stone and terracotta grinders in PGW assemblages indicate the preparation of food grains of some kind.

Only the limited use of iron is suggested for these village populations at the turn of the second and first millennia BC. At Bhagwanpura, as has been seen, the grey pottery levels yielded no iron at all, but at other, probably later sites tools such as arrowheads, spearheads, axes, nails, knives, sickles, tongs and pins have been found. The local manufacture of these objects is attested to by the presence of slag and small fragments of iron.

Although the great cities of the Ganges plains were the direct descendants of the Iron Age villages invariably found stratified under them, in common with the Indus Civilisation of many centuries before they were not the only kind of settlement of the period. The small, Iron Age villages typified by the presence of grey pottery or black and red pottery were the ancestors of a profusion of small villages of the later periods. Often the archaeology of ancient India has concentrated upon large and more dramatic sites to the inevitable exclusion of the village settlement. With advances in exploration in both India and Pakistan a profusion of pre-urban sites containing grey pottery has been found. The precise relationship of these sites to the variety of cultures preceding them is not in every case clear. A very convincing connection is recognisable, however, between grey pottery villages at sites in the Indian Punjab and the late Harappan and between Iron Age sites bearing the same later grey wares and the great cities of the Ganges plains.

By about 600 BC a change took place from a purely village culture to the beginning of urban life in north India. Settlements grew in size and complexity, and the character of the material culture found in them began to alter in kind and in quality. A novel form of *de luxe* ceramic ware was introduced at about this time. This is the famous Northern Black Polished ware, or NBP as it is usually called. This pottery has, typically, a black glossy surface and a fine, well-prepared body. Although it is found in a wide variety of shapes, NBP assumed the two classic forms of the preceding Painted Grey Ware, the shallow tray-bowl and high-sided cup.

The transition from the simple villages of the Iron Age to the complexities of early civilised life in north India was not sudden, nor were all traces of the earlier style of village lost at that time. There is evidence for a survival of earlier ceramic wares into the city period, hardly surprising in a culture where conservatism is often a basic principle. The rise of cities in the Ganges area was accompanied by a rise in the number of small settlements associated with them. In most cases these villages could not have changed their basic style of rural existence to any great extent. The complexities of urban culture bore down on these villages affecting everything from religion to material possessions and economy. The basic principles of the simple life of the village cultivator can hardly have altered in any real way, however. The day-to-day problems of earning a living faced these small settlements as starkly then as they have during succeeding centuries.

By the middle of the last millennium BC, for reasons that are not clear, certain small Iron Age villages on the vast flood plains of the Ganges had grown into large, complex centres of population surrounded, typically, by massive defen-

A section of the ramparts of the ancient city of Mathura on the Jamuna River.

sive walls and giving evidence of all the attributes of a developed and intricate cultural system. At sites such as Kausambi, Mathura, Sravasti, Hastinapur, Ahichchhatra and many others the tiny pre-urban settlement is swamped by the magnitude of the later arrangement. These developments took place all over north India from east to west and into the peninsula.

During this second flowering of city life in the subcontinent foundations were laid for the basic village–city relationship that has existed in India ever since. There is no break in the archaeological sequence from then until the present day to suggest that the idea of the city and the culture associated with it either declined or vanished, as was the case for the Indus Civilisation. Most of the great cities of north India suffered terribly in one way or another, often being laid waste through invasion or neglect. In no case, however, did such destruction of the physical structure of city life mean that the principles upon which it had been developed were lost. The expansion of population in the years following the growth of these Ganges cities in association with a solidly founded literary, political, religious and artistic tradition was enough to preserve the basics of civilisation. In any case, the great geographical diversity of this new city-oriented culture meant that where it could not survive in one area it did in another. The cities of the Ganges Civilisation, as it might be called, are the direct ancestors of their modern counterparts and, in some cases, are found in deposits stratified under them.

These centuries are full of the most important developments: coinage was introduced in the form of cast copper and punch-marked silver; writing was

Two gold staters (diam. 2cm) of the Gupta monarch, Chandragupta II (reigned AD 382–414).

developed, probably at about this time as well, although the first inscriptions are not known until the reign of the Emperor Ashoka some 200 years later. This early style of writing is known as Brahmi and is the direct ancestor of the modern Indian scripts. Religion, politics, law, the arts, town planning, trade, communications, warfare and every other aspect of ordinary life developed in complexity at this time.

Associated with these developments within the great walls of the urban centres was an increase in population and a spread of people across north India bringing with them the principles of Vedic civilisation. The movement of these people is recorded in the literature of the period which provides much information about other aspects of life. The caste system began to develop in the centuries before the first cities, becoming a basic part of Indian society to the present day. Land was put to the plough, and crops such as wheat, barley, millet and rice were grown. The usual range of Indian domestic animals was present as well. Various metals, including iron and bronze, were known in these cities, and craft specialisation grew in complexity as surpluses, particularly of food, allowed for a more diversified economy based on trade.

Typically, the cities of this period are very large. Kausambi, near Allahabad, is nearly eight kilometres in circuit. Usually situated near one of the great rivers of the plains, these cities are surrounded by moats and massive walls of burnt brick pierced by gates at regular intervals. At Kausambi eleven gates are known. These walls served both the purposes of defence and, probably, flood protection. Regrettably, no single city site of the last centuries BC has ever been extensively excavated horizontally. Work has most often been limited to determination of the material sequence at these sites. The result is that internal town organisation is known only in small part for this period. There is no separation of citadel and lower town as was true for the cities of the Indus. Religion, politics, administration and the daily life of the ordinary city dweller all took place within the great walls of the urban centre.

Temples and monumental buildings were built in these cities. Domestic architecture was usually constructed in baked brick or stone and included houses with many rooms and courtyards. Systems of domestic and communal drains were used along with wells lined with multi-sectioned terracotta collars, and 'soakage pits' of large jars set one on top of the other. Within these cities as great centres of population there were, presumably, market-places with specialised areas for the different crafts.

Plan of the ancient city of Kausambi on the Jamuna River near Allahabad, drawn and published in the 19th century by General Cunningham, Director-General of the Archaeological Survey of India. The site is some 8 km in circuit.

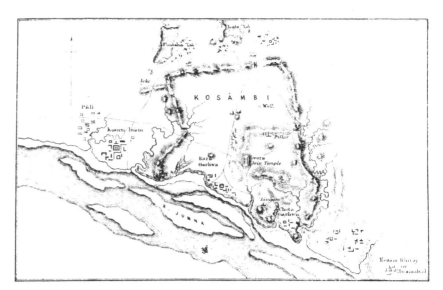

A panel from the stupa at Amaravati in Andhra Pradesh showing a procession of men, horses and elephants passing through an elaborate gate of a great city wall. BM 1880. 7–9. 19.

The Buddha, Gupta period, *c.* 5th–6th century AD. BM 1880–6.

The relationship between the urban centres and villages of the period is not archaeologically defined, but it can be assumed that any small settlement in the vicinity of a large and powerful city would have been influenced by it. Goods and services of various kinds would have been exchanged between the various villages and towns in any given area with the main centre of distribution being the largest. The extent to which the residents of any large urban centre relied upon rural settlements for subsistence is a problem yet unsolved. In all probability certain sections of any urban population cultivated fields adjacent to the city or even, although the archaeological record does not reveal it, within the walls, as open space would permit such activity.

From the standpoint of the political history of ancient India the cities of the Ganges served an important purpose. With the decline of what may be styled 'tribal' life in north India under pressure from the spread of Vedic culture, the growth of political units of often very large size began. By the middle of the first millennium BC the foundations of the great independent republics and kingdoms of north India had been laid. These *mahajanapadas*, as they were called, were at the basis of the political structure of ancient India. The great cities of the Ganges were the main or subsidiary capitals of these units: Kausambi was the main city of the Vatsas, Rajgir of Magadha, Sravasti of Kosala, Ahichchhatra of the northern Panchalas, and so on. These states varied in power and influence: Magadha, in particular, with its capital first in the fortress valley at Rajgir and later at Pataliputra on the Ganges, became the centre of the greatest political unity ever known in India. From the fourth century BC to the death of the Emperor Ashoka in 232 BC the Mauryan empire centred in Magadha controlled territory from Kandahar to Orissa and deep into south India.

The rise of the great new religions of the period, Buddhism and Jainism, took place within the context of the structure of these states and capitals. The Buddha (*c.* 560–480 BC) was, before his enlightenment, prince of a small state in what is now part of the *Terai* region of southern Nepal and northern India. His life consisted largely of a series of journeys between the cities of the middle Ganges region and various periods of residence in many of them. The further history of ancient India is one of a series of dynastic hegemonies, none of them ever again as extensive as that of the Mauryas but each of them noteworthy, particularly for their achievements in the arts and literature.

As the political structure of these cities and states grew in complexity, the formulation of principles of administrative behaviour began in written form. The laws of Manu and the Arthashastra of Kautilya, the Machiavelli of ancient India, are two of the most important texts of the early city period. Compilation of the two great epic poems of ancient India, the *Mahabharata* and the *Ramayana*, took place likewise at that time. Principles of grammar, architecture and city planning and the arts were similarly established. The basis, in short, of classical Indian culture as it has been transmitted to the present day is to be sought in the cities of the plains of north India. Parallel, yet somewhat later, cultural developments took place in south India. The growth of the classic culture of the Tamils at about the turn of the Christian era is marked by the rise of the famous literature of the monasteries or Sangams.

Communications between the cities of north India were by river and road. Little is known of ships of the period, but land transport of goods and people involved the use of bullock-drawn carts, camels and elephants. The ancient literature speaks of well-used routes across north India and from the north to the south of the subcontinent. Trade and commerce within the Indian culture area were extensive; trade with the world outside the subcontinent also took place, as the evidence of contacts with the Greek and Roman empires and other parts of the ancient world attest. As the centuries passed, the cultural influence of India grew in extent expanding far afield to affect in many basic ways the civilisations of other parts of Asia – South-East Asia in particular. Through the spread of the

A bracket carved in the image of a Salabhanjika, a female forest deity, from Sonkh near Mathura, *c.* 2nd century AD.

Buddhist religion nearly every part of Asia came to regard India as, to some extent, a spiritual centre. Buddhist pilgrims faced tremendous odds in their journeys to the places associated with the life of their great teacher.

The arts grew in range and quality during this early historic period. In the villages of Iron Age India artistic expression was limited, as far as is known, to the decoration of pottery and the manufacture of small objects of terracotta. By the time of the Mauryas the classical three-dimensional arts of ancient India were well established. The stone sculpture of the Mauryas is of a character and a quality scarcely equalled in subsequent periods. As in all Indian sculpture, the themes are religious, taking subjects from Buddhism in particular. Mauryan sculpture is monumental and is made exclusively from a kind of buff sandstone which was subsequently given a characteristic high polish. The famous lion capitol from Sarnath, the symbol of the modern Indian republic, is the best-known example of this style. It was originally mounted at the summit of a high pillar, also in polished sandstone, one of many erected in north India at the time of the Emperor Ashoka. Inscriptions on these pillars and on prominent rocky eminences promulgate Ashoka's belief in the truth of the Buddhist law.

By the last century or two BC Indian three-dimensional art and architecture flourished magnificently. Among the greatest monuments are the great stupas of Barhut and Sanchi which date from the Sunga dynasty (c. 187–75 BC). A stupa is a dome-like monument of solid masonry erected over a collection of cremated relics contained in a small casket of stone or metal. At these two sites the decorative instincts of the ancient Indian artist knew no limits. The railings and gateway surrounding the monuments at Barhut and Sanchi are all sculpted in the most exquisite and detailed fashion with scenes in the life of the Buddha or other associated symbols or conventions. The stupa at Barhut is preserved now as a collection of sculptures housed at various museums in India, but the complex at Sanchi is among the world's most magnificent monuments testifying to the skill and refinement of the Indian artist and to the appreciation of these qualities on the part of the patrons of such art, the inhabitants of the great cities of ancient India.

The beauty of the reliefs at the great stupa at Amaravati in the modern state of Andhra Pradesh should not be ignored. Dating from the centuries surrounding the turn of the Christian era, the Buddhist sculptures at Amaravati exhibit at once a spirituality and a quality of humanity seldom equalled anywhere. From the sculpted panels at Amaravati, Sanchi, Barhut and Mathura much of what is known of the architecture of the ancient cities has been derived. Scenes depicting high city walls, elaborate portals and gateways, edifices with complex gabling and religious buildings, stupas and temples are all found in these reliefs. The cities of ancient India were clearly monumental and imposing, a fitting backdrop to the great events of the centuries during which they were built. Alongside these city walls the reliefs at Amaravati and Sanchi depict the thatched huts of the village farmer. They show him resting at the plough along with his livestock or worshipping at the sacred places of his religion. As ever, the juxtaposition of the rural and the urban is the Indian settlement principle, the mass of the population living in the villages.

The daily life of the ordinary city dweller of 2,000 years ago cannot have differed much in its basic principles from that of his rural cousins. The caste system circumscribed his occupation. Although particular trades or crafts, in so far as they may have been performed exclusively within the urban context, dictated that certain aspects of ordinary life differed from those of the villager, in most ways they can hardly have differed at all. Most people must have used plain red pottery vessels for cooking or eating and, in keeping with the basic tenets of whatever their religion may have been, worshipped regularly at small village shrines or at larger temples in the cities.

A railing cross-bar from the stupa at Amaravati depicting a scene of elaborate court life with nobles entertained by a large group of female dancers and musicians.
BM 1880. 7–9. 12.

The life of the rich and privileged in these ancient times presents a much more elaborate picture. The matchless frescoes at Ajanta in western India give a glimpse of the exotic richness of courtly life as it was imagined to have been lived by the Buddha before his departure from his father's palace. The elaborate personal adornment of female figures made in terracotta speak of prosperity and luxury.

The Hindu religion developed into what became ultimately the basic belief of most Indians. It grew out of a combination of Brahmanical beliefs and native customs influenced by Buddhism, Jainism and various religious revivals. Even during the periods when Buddhism was the official religion of various states of the subcontinent the worship of Brahmanical gods and goddesses and practice of the caste system were ever present. The cities of ancient India contained a

A magnificently attired female figure,
a terracotta plaque found at Tamluk
near the mouth of the Ganges,
c. 2nd–1st century BC.

A pair of terracotta female figurines from the excavations at Mathura, probably representing a form of mother goddess, *c.* 3rd–2nd century BC.

A richly carved pillar from the ancient city site at Eran on the Bina River in Madhya Pradesh District, *c.* 5th–6th century AD.

considerable religious variety, therefore, and it is no surprise to find in them images in stone or terracotta of both Buddhist and Hindu deities. The great cave temples of India, mostly in western India, with temples hewn out of the solid rock, are monuments to all the religions of ancient India. The richness of these temples is a monument likewise to both the artistry and devotion of the sculptors and to the economic strength of the city-based society that was its inspiration and patron.

By the time of the Gupta dynasty in the fourth to sixth centuries AD the height of city-based culture in north India had been reached. Great religious monuments full of exquisite stone or terracotta sculpture had been built both at the places of pilgrimage and in the cities themselves. The cities and such great monasteries as that founded in Nalanda in modern Bihar flourished all over the land, attracting students of religion to them from many parts of the ancient world. Metalwork flourished, and the production of religious images in bronze began to develop into both a great industry and a great art. The arts, particularly sculpture, developed a characteristic style that was to influence the arts of all of Indianised Asia. With the coming of the White Huns to north India these Gupta cities fell into decline and the great monasteries were neglected to be revived in the eighth century under the patronage of the Bengali Pala kings. As ever, village settlements endured.

CHAPTER EIGHT

The later monasteries

Crowned Buddha, a stone panel in high relief found at the Pala period monastery site at Antichak near Bhagalpur on the Ganges River. This sculpture is a fine example of the last flowering of Buddhist art in India and the richness of the monastery complexes that contained it.

The period between the eighth and twelfth centuries AD was the traditional golden age of Bengal. During this period in what is now Bihar, west Bengal and Bangladesh a revival of Buddhist art took place in concert with the political stability of the Pala kingdom and the direct patronage of its rulers. This period saw the last flowering of the Buddhist religion and its art before its ultimate absorption into Hinduism. Great monasteries were founded by the Pala kings. The first of the rulers, Gopala, was said to have revived the great teaching monastery at Nalanda and established several new religious centres. The second Pala king, Dharmapala, built the famous Vikramshila Mahavihara, the site of which is now thought to be the ruins at Antichak in Bhagalpur District, Bihar. It is said that fifty other monasteries were erected by Dharmapala specifically for the study of the teachings of his spiritual guide, Haribhadra, whose disciple, Buddhajnanapada, became the first head of the Vikramshila monastery. Scholars flocked to this centre from many parts of the ancient Buddhist world, particularly Tibet. This eastern Indian form of tantric Buddhism has a profound influence on the religion of Tibet and its artistic expression.

Tibetan and Chinese records preserve nearly all that is traditionally known about these great monasteries. It is said that in the eleventh century AD there were 160 teachers and some 1,000 monks at Antichak in the Mahavihara, or great monastery. As only 208 monastic cells have been discovered at Antichak, presumably these were used by the teachers and the huge number of students resided in temporary shelters outside the monastery walls. Similarly, at Nalanda only a very limited number of permanent monastic residences are known archaeologically. The thousands of students who are reported to have flocked there cannot have lived in the complex itself. An administrative board composed of eminent teachers supervised the affairs of both the monasteries at Vikramshila and Nalanda. Other great centres such as the Somapura monastery at Paharpur and the Pattikera at Mainamati, both in Bangladesh, functioned similarly as centres of learning. Like the others, they were rich and extensive establishments, the setting for the growth of a distinctive eastern Indian art style in sculpture, writing and manuscript painting.

The university at Antichak consists of a square compound some 330 m on each side. The cells of the monks at this complex were built into this perimeter wall and were 208 in number. Each cell has a bed platform, and underground cells beneath them may have served for meditation. The principal entrance to the monastery was an imposing gate on the north side of the complex complete with stairs and with a roof held up by pillars over a brick-paved avenue. At the centre of the monastery compound was an imposing cruciform edifice built of baked brick, the principal monument at Antichak, and was, probably, a stupa with two terraces. On the level of both of the terraces a series of terracotta plaques depicting an endless variety of Buddhist symbolism was set into the wall of the shrine. As many as 2,800 of these plaques were found at Paharpur. Small temples and votive stupas of varying sizes are also associated with these

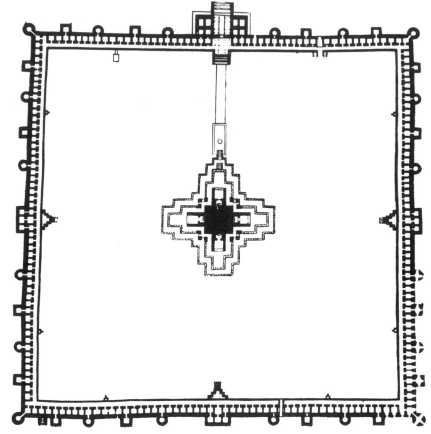

Ground plan of the great monastery at Antichak, said to be the famous Vikramshila Mahavihara. At the centre is a stupa built on a series of cruciform platforms. The perimeter wall contains the cells of the monks. The complex is 330 m square.

great complexes. In the walls of the central shrines are niches meant for images of the Buddha in both bronze and stone.

At Nalanda the use of stucco for religious sculpture is widespread. Visited by the Chinese pilgrim Hiuen Tsang in the seventh century AD, Nalanda was a great centre of learning. He reports that 'Learned men from different cities, who desire to acquire quickly a renown in discussion, come here [Nalanda] in multitudes to settle their doubts, and then the streams [of their wisdom] spread far and wide. For this reason some persons usurp the name [of Nalanda students], and in going to and fro receive honour in consequence'.

On a day-to-day level the domestic material assemblage of the monks at Antichak or any other of these establishments varied only little from the material known at sites of the earlier cities. Vessels of pottery and bronze were used. High stands held, presumably, small terracotta lamps to illuminate the monks' cells. Seals and finger rings of bronze as well as endless small clay pots, possibly of some ritual character, have been found at these cities. Cowrie shells were used as currency, large quantities of which have been found at Antichak. The monks were most likely vegetarians and relied upon the produce of local village farms for subsistence. The large number of students and teachers at any of the great monasteries would require the supply of vast quantities of food. The royal subsidies that supported these establishments must have been used in large part to that end.

There are better contemporary descriptions of the University at Nalanda than for any other. Hiuen Tsang goes into some detail and describes a complex of monastic cells, courtyards, stupas, Buddha images large and small, and monuments to relics of the Buddha. Among the latter sort was a stupa containing remains of the Buddha's hair and nails. Hiuen Tsang says: 'Those persons afflicted with complicated diseases, coming here and turning round religiously, are mostly healed.' Near by was a tree two to three metres high, allegedly the Buddha's toothbrush, which took root after he flung it down on the ground. As well as images of the Buddha, statues of various deities of the Buddhist pantheon were erected at Nalanda or in the vicinity of the monastery. Hiuen Tsang describes a large figure of the Bodhisattva Tara, allegedly of great height: 'Every fast-day of the year large offerings are made to it. The kings and ministers and great people of the neighbouring countries offer exquisite per-fumes and flowers, holding gem-covered flags and canopies, whilst instru-ments of metal and stone resound in turns, mingled with the harmony of flutes and harps. These religious assemblies last for seven days.'

To complete the general impression created by the monastery complex at Nalanda a final word from Hiuen Tsang:

The whole establishment is surrounded by a brick wall. One gate opens into the great college, from which are separated eight other halls, standing in the middle (of the *sanghārāma*).

The richly adorned towers and the fairy-like turrets, like the pointed hill-tops, are congregated together. The observations seem to be lost in the vapour (of the morning) and the upper rooms tower above the sky.

From the windows one may see how the winds and the clouds (produce new forms), and above the soaring eaves the conjunctions of the sun and moon (may be observed).

All outside courts, in which are the priests' chambers, are of four stages. The stages have dragon projections and coloured eaves, the pearl-red pillars carved and ornamented, the richly adorned balustrades, and the roofs covered with tiles that reflect the light in a thousand shades. These things add to the beauty of the place.

An image in stucco of the Buddha in teaching posture from the great monastery at Nalanda. A Gupta foundation, this centre flourished later with the support of the Pala dynasty.

These ancient universities were active and stimulating places and, heavily subsidied by the Pala monarchs, were adorned with a profusion of religious images in every medium. The tantric Buddhism of the Pala period encouraged the worship of various godheads, and through the necessity to visualise these entities vast quantities of images of gods and Buddhas in many forms were made. Bronze and black stone are the two characteristic sculptural media of the period. The style is characterised by a delicacy of intricate carving in high relief and of intense spirituality. The stylistic influence of this Pala school of art and the religion that dominated it is seen in Tibet and Nepal, in Burma and in Java. Images of both Buddhist and Hindu deities are known from this period.

As well as sculpture in metal and stone votive objects in terracotta are characteristic of the great monasteries of the Pala kingdom. Seals minutely inscribed with the Buddhist creed or other texts, small inscribed plaques bearing images of the Buddha in low relief, and small votive stupas containing pairs of stamped inscriptions are among the most typical of these remains.

These complex university sites of the eastern Ganges plains are a far cry from the small cluster of Mesolithic huts that is the first known settlement in north India. They typify a truly varied and complicated civilisation possessed of a unique and original style of art and great philosophical profundity. They represent a peak of sophistication and innovation and bear the hallmarks of a great tradition of learning and artistic expression. During this period, as throughout the millennia-long growth of settlements in India, the villages remained the basic unit of population and can have differed in hardly any fundamental detail from small villages in modern Bihar and Bengal. The tenacity of village culture as a very broad concept is once more revealed in eastern India. With the downfall of the Pala dynasty began the decline of Buddhism as a classical culture influencing most aspects of life in the areas of its domination. By the fourteenth century it had disappeared for good as an indigenous religion, only to be revived in recent times. The great monasteries and cities of Bihar and Bengal fell into neglect and ruin, but the farming villages that supported these grand centres remained.

The serpent goddess Manasa, from eastern India, 9th century AD. A profusion of metal images of the highest quality is one characteristic of the art of the Pala monastery. BM 1936. 2–11. 1.

In so many ways the country village has been the backbone of Indian culture. This can be seen even in the way that aspects of classical culture and tradition can be preserved and handed on by word of mouth by 'illiterate' villagers from one millennia to the next. Regard for the importance of the Indian village and its farmer inhabitants has long informed Indian thought: there is a classical account of a battle raging, and not far from it a village farmer peacefully continues tilling his field, safe from the ravages of war. The timeless institution of the Indian village survives, despite the great events of history, and should be seen in its myriad forms in all parts of the subcontinent, to be at the foundation of Indian culture.

PART TWO

VASNA: VILLAGE LIFE IN GUJARAT

Brian Durrans

Rabari herdsmen waiting by the tank for a truck to collect the morning's milk. Beyond lie the fields with a scatter of trees, and the National Highway.

CHAPTER ONE
Introduction

South-west of Ahmedabad, the largest city in Gujarat, the flat panorama is broken by scattered groups of trees. Older people can remember parties of sahibs coming here for the wildfowling in the 1930s when the land was more wooded and gave good cover. The woods have since given way to open fields and roads; harvests are bigger and more reliable, transport is easier, and most people are glad of the change. But a price has been paid: there is now no source of firewood, and cow-dung is used as fuel instead of being recycled as manure. Farmers therefore resort to expensive chemical fertilisers. This problem illustrates the close dependence of the village on its immediate surroundings and the chain-reaction effect of change on traditional ways.

The Indian villager inherits two kinds of tradition: one, from the distant past, determines the layout of the house and the village and the main contours of social and religious life; the other, emerging from more recent history and still influential, conditions, modifies and adds detail to this basic framework. Such a view is, of course, an over-simplification, but it fits the Gujarati evidence reasonably well. It should be emphasised, however, that no society or community passively accepts change from outside. Whether it changes much or hardly at all is decided by its own internal dynamics, by the options which people recognise. In India the way society operates at village level tends to discourage structural change. The dominant feature of village life is the exceptionally tight integration between economy, society and beliefs which is achieved by the caste system. This is the main factor which conserves tradition.

The following account of village life in part of central Gujarat gives a local focus to these generalisations. Based on limited personal acquaintance, it presents a selective introduction to a complex and fascinating subject. By interpreting some aspects of the historical background of local culture the debt of the present to the past should be made clear, and by describing part of the contemporary experience of the villages it should be recognised that this is also of interest in its own right. No village in India can be described as typical, and Gujarati villages are as distinctive as any in the whole country. Nevertheless, details about life in one small part of rural India can give reality to that elusive abstraction 'the Indian village'.

Cow-dung cakes, bearing the imprint of the hands that shaped them, drying on a wall in the sun. When they are dry they fall off ready for use as fuel.

CHAPTER TWO

Vasna: the present

A school classroom in use. Teachers, themselves often from the village community, help transmit a wider, national outlook to the rising generation, but some children may have to miss lessons to help their hard-pressed parents in the fields.

The village referred to here as Vasna does not exist; it is a convenient fiction used to typify a group of about a dozen villages which are situated in the Sabarmati River basin to the south and south-west of Ahmedabad. Any one of these villages differs from Vasna only in minor detail; Vasna therefore could exist and will be assumed to exist in the following account. The information presented here, which was collected in the field, derives from several villages, and the fabrication of Vasna protects their anonymity. Nothing reported is invention, however, it is a composite of details true of one village or another.

Agriculture

The village boundaries enclose about 1,500 hectares of brown-black saline soil. Average annual rainfall in this part of Gujarat is about 120 cm. This is seasonal, unreliable and insufficient for padi rice cultivation, the main subsistence activity. Irrigation is therefore the basis of the local economy. Water is supplied to the fields in two main ways: from deep tube wells and from the Sabarmati via a vast network of canals. The Moti Fatewadi canal is one of the most ambitious engineering projects ever undertaken in the area. Started shortly before Independence, it has been extended so that it now irrigates nearly 13,500 hectares. The tube wells descend to about 180 m, but the water they provide is salty and exacerbates the existing soil salinity.

Women threshing rice cover their faces as protection against flying chaff. Working in a group helps reduce the tedium of this exhausting task.

Grown on about a third of all the land under cultivation, rice is a relatively new feature in local agriculture. Thirty years ago villagers had not yet broken free of the fear of famine, which in varying degree had formed part of regional experience for hundreds and perhaps thousands of years. Rice was not only a newly dominant cereal which could not have been grown successfully on this scale before irrigation; it was the first reliable staple. For this dramatic improvement villagers know they must thank local and national government institutions and advanced forms of technology, but now that the change has been achieved, the rice is cultivated mainly by means of existing village techniques and equipment. Only fertilisers and insecticides are new additions to the farmer's traditional means of production, although the few who can afford it may sometimes use tractors.

The village has about six small grocery stores, a post office, school and one telephone owned by a local co-operative society. Of the village population of about 2,000 in nearly 400 households, over 90 per cent are Hindus, the remainder Muslims. High-caste Rajputs, Patels and Harijan (formerly Untouchable) Vankars make up over half of all households and between them own most of the land. The Vankars are members of the weaver-caste, but only about half continue weaving, and most of these spend as much or more of their time in the fields as at the loom. This is because weaving is relatively unrewarding, a point which will be examined in more detail later. Although these three castes comprise the majority of households, they are only a bare minority of cultivators, the majority of whom therefore work less than half the available land.

57

Most families of all castes own at least some land, but there are still noticeable differences in ownership within and between castes. In addition, as much land as the Rajputs have (about 400 hectares) is owned and cultivated by relatively well-off farmers living in near-by villages where they have other holdings. There are altogether about 450 land-owning farmers in Vasna. Inequality is not extreme, however; half the land under cultivation in Vasna is farmed in plots of between two and six hectares, and most of the remainder is in smallholdings. These 'middle' farmers own more land than either the relatively rich or relatively poor cultivators.

Where some people have insufficient land to engage their full attention and others have more than they can manage on their own, there is scope for the former to work for the latter, and in Vasna this operates in accordance with traditional caste practice of payment in kind. There are also about 300 landless labourers in the village to perform this work, though at critical times such as harvesting these may be augmented by itinerant labourers from outside the village who may be paid in cash.

The problem facing the smallholder is a serious one: land-ownership is the traditional measure of economic security in village India. To divide a small piece of land between several sons may benefit each only slightly, yet for one alone to inherit is to dispossess the others. The only escape from this dilemma is to seek alternative kinds of security, such as pensionable jobs. This usually entails leaving the village for the town or city. There are proud fathers in Vasna whose sons work in offices in the nearest town, and at least one weaver's son works in a Bombay bank.

The relatively larger, but still modest areas of land owned by some villagers may seem to confer an offensively unfair advantage over their poorer neighbours. The generally high level of agricultural productivity and the caste system itself effectively limit the impact of this inequality on the smallholder. Even a small piece of land, provided it is adequately irrigated, can yield a good return on the seed and work invested. Not only caste ideology but also a common interest in maintaining high selling prices further reduce the risk of conflict between these groups. All groups know that differences of wealth and power within the village are relatively slight compared with those which exist in the world outside. Some of these differences are reported in sensationalist terms, as when newspapers or magazines announce film-stars' earnings; but company profits and wage levels in Ahmedabad or Baroda will be discussed with as much interest. Greater involvement in city life, education and the advent of mass communications have enabled the villagers to get their own experience into perspective, while the absence of extreme deprivation frees them from the temptation automatically to blame their relatively wealthier immediate neighbours for their own misfortune. Participation in electoral politics has also had the effect of turning people's attention to issues beyond the village.

Although padi is the main crop, others are still important. Against nearly 400 hectares given over to rice, more than 300 hectares are reserved for cotton grown for cash, while millets (*jowar* and *bajri*), grown mainly for cattle fodder, take up about 300 hectares. Wheat has been displaced by rice and now occupies only about 160 hectares. Much smaller areas are devoted to cash crops such as sugar-cane, caster or mustard, to vegetable cultivation and to green fodder. Most farmers limit themselves to food and fodder crops, for their own use and where possible for sale; but specialised cash cropping is more the prerogative of those with larger holdings.

One weaver with a modest two hectares plans his cultivation cycle as follows, and his routine is conventional: during December and January insecticides are applied to the growing winter wheat which was sown in November; this is harvested in February. At the beginning of March he sows bajri for harvesting at the end of April. Vegetables put in immediately afterwards are available before June when the land is fertilised. In July the padi is sown, and over the following weeks transplanted and later treated with insecticides until it ripens in November.

The use of fertiliser in this regime compensates for the absence of a full crop rotation system. Systematic rotation including legumes would be cheaper than buying commercial fertiliser, but this overlooks the tight squeeze on both space and seasonal time which the three main crops impose. The seasonal factor is vital: it is not just a matter of agricultural logic, for the whole organisation of village life is seasonal. Winter crops (*rabi*) of millets and wheat (and vegetables) complement the monsoon crop (*kharif*) of padi, and there is no room in between to vary the pattern. The farmer uses ten extra men to help him during the most labour-intensive phases, for sowing and harvesting the main crops and for transplanting the padi, but he applies fertiliser and insecticides and does most of the ploughing himself with a pair of water-buffaloes.

By a brick-built store-house facing his fields, this weaver/farmer has a concrete-lined well from which he pumps water to irrigate his land as required. By local standards he makes a good living, but he works very hard and finds time to pursue his relatively unrewarding traditional occupation only when the cultivation cycle permits. Although two hectares is not much, most weavers have less.

A landless labourer.

Village structure

The form of village settlement between Ahmedabad and the town of Dholka is a linear cluster resembling others in central and northern Gujarat. This looks like the *pol* arrangement of houses, seen in the urban areas of the region, which greatly impressed European visitors during the sixteenth century and later.

An unkempt byre in a corner of a khadki. Both bullocks and water-buffaloes are used for traction, and buffaloes are also milked.

The houses of the same caste community are built in a terrace, and a pair of such rows face each other across a more or less narrow yard, shared for communal activities, which resembles a street but does not normally receive through traffic. Between the open yard and the front door of each house there is often, but not always, a narrow veranda raised a few centimetres above the level of the yard itself and sometimes partly screened behind a low mud wall. The whole dwelling complex, known as a *khadki*, is enclosed within a continuous barrier comprising the rear walls of all the component houses.

A yard in a weavers' khadki. On the left wooden winding-frames for cotton yarn hang suspended from wall pegs above string cots (charpoys) stacked on their sides.

In practice this format is modified by special restrictions which are imposed by the size of the caste community, the phase of village development when the community joined it, the arrangements of other castes, and so on. One notable difference between the typical north Gujarat khadki as described and that found in Vasna is that the back walls of weavers' houses in Vasna have doors and windows, although the doors are generally smaller than those at the front. Occasionally a door or window may be found in the side wall of an end house. The reason for this departure from the classic pattern is probably the need to allow sufficient light into the weaver's workshop to enable him to operate the loom. Neither lamps nor electric lights are powerful or cheap enough as alternatives. This is especially important during hot weather when the weaver usually prefers to work very early in the morning. Unless suitably positioned to receive light from a low sun, the loom will be hard to use at this time.

There is no strict rule, but usually the weaver occupies the rear room while women's work and the hearth are confined to the front. Again, this is a departure from the orthodox scheme of north Gujarat, and the reason for it seems to be connected with the practical needs of the weaver and with changes in village life. Once a door is provided in the back or side wall to admit light, it can also be used to enter and leave the workshop independently of the front room. This in turn allows the space allocated to women to continue to be used exclusively by them at times of heightened danger of ritual pollution, as during menstruation or childbirth. Traditionally, an unperforated rear wall was necessary for security against raids by outsiders, but life in Vasna is now safer than in the past. A family who maintain the classic allocation of front room for weaving and rear room for cooking and eating may therefore only be taking advantage of the orientation of their house. To have no door or window in the back wall does not mean the householder feels vulnerable to theft. The significance of occupation in this respect is indicated by the fact that basket-makers (*bhangis*) and potters (*kumbhars*), who work outside, have no need to add doors and windows in this way or to vary the traditional allocation of rooms.

Another difference between the weavers' quarter in Vasna and the classic khadki is the absence of a gateway at one end of the shared yard. This feature is mainly a security measure in larger, richer villages, towns and cities, and its absence in Vasna probably reflects the relative poverty of the village and of the weavers in particular.

The village consists of several khadki enclosures, the position and detailed arrangement of each reflecting the particular stage at which it originally joined in the evolution of the total settlement. The location of a village was originally constrained by the need for drinking water and suitable mud for house-building. Founding a village on the site of an earlier,one was tempting because the mud in existing walls could be recycled. Village ponds, later to become tanks or reservoirs, were created incidentally when mud was excavated from a low-lying area to construct a village on a new site.

If the village prospered and grander houses began to be built, the pond (*bhagol*) or several ponds would become the source of material for bricks. Whatever the size or prosperity of the village, the bhagol is the only zone open to all inhabitants. Otherwise each individual properly belongs only to the house of his family and to the khadki of his local caste community. The bhagol and the village well are generally located slightly away from the houses so that they can be used by members of different castes without the risk of ritual pollution of inhabited areas. It would be inconvenient to have to clean such areas thoroughly following a case of ritual pollution, as required by traditional caste practice. Quite apart from this, they are set where possible on higher ground so that waste water will not percolate into the built area. This counters both ritual and sanitary pollution.

A mother washes her daughter on a discarded millstone which inclines towards a bottomless clay jar, buried in the ground, acting as a soak-pit.

The supply of water, the one shared resource of the whole village in traditional times before the private ownership of wells, influenced architecture and daily routines as well as the initial choice of village site. The use of lime plaster in house construction is very rare because it would have been socially unacceptable for one village family to appropriate for itself the prodigious quantity of water required. The economic importance of water gave it a powerful symbolic role in traditional thought, and it was particularly symbolic of village unity.

Fetching water remains women's work; it is carried on the head in round-bottomed red earthenware pots or in more angular brass vessels, often one stacked on top of the other. The effort of bringing it to the house and the general absence of domestic washing facilities, as much as any shortage in the well itself, have encouraged the practice of washing as close as possible to the source of the water, the well or bhagol, or at least in an area away from the khadki. Nowadays in Vasna these considerations do not always apply, but care is taken that the water used for these purposes is retained in a vessel for disposal later or runs off immediately away from the house. Often a discarded millstone is placed on a slightly raised part of the yard or inclined away from any near-by house to be used as a platform on which young children may be washed by their mothers, or for adults to perform their ablutions. Beneath this platform a bottomless clay jar is buried which serves as a soak-pit – a practice which has a long antiquity in India.

Caste and ritual pollution

If caste is the central institution in traditional Indian village life, then the concept of pollution is the central element in caste. This concept links caste ideology with social practice.

Castes are exclusive, hierarchically ranked but mutually interdependent groups. Each caste in Vasna occupies its own residential area and carries out, at least nominally, its own inherited traditional occupation. Inter-caste marriage remains rare, but there are occasions on which collaboration is encouraged. Certain rituals or festivals, political meetings, or the marriage or funeral of an important villager may attract participation by members of several castes, although it will always be clear from the way groups keep apart that rules are not totally relaxed. However, most routine relations between castes are bilateral – the exchange of goods or services according to traditional precepts, where the basis of the relationship is inequality and continuity.

In the ideal village the main requirements of life may be conveniently provided for everyone by having all main caste groups present. The more isolated a village is, the more necessary for the ideal scheme to be followed. In Vasna, which was never very isolated and is certainly not isolated today, it has been sufficient for the wide spectrum of castes to be augmented in near-by villages or towns. This binds neighbouring settlements closer together.

The spread of members of the same caste through different villages has always been an important feature of rural life. Such distributions allow hospitality and other obligations to be widely reciprocated even when individuals do not know each other personally, which is especially useful when religious pilgrimages are made or when festivals or fairs are attended far from home. Such links have always existed, but one of the major changes of modern times in Vasna is that regular public transport and better roads allow them to be used more often.

Relations between members of different castes are governed by clear rules for the avoidance of ritual pollution of higher by lower caste members. *Ritual* pollution is something quite different from kinds of pollution occurring in other contexts: it presupposes a set of ideas concerning the relationship between spiritual and physical life. For the orthodox Hindu, pollution is a threat to one's spiritual well-being, to be cancelled by some form of purification ritual. The origin of this threat is a person of lower caste than oneself, and the greater the difference of rank, the greater the threat, reaching the ultimate in the ritual danger to the highest-ranking Brahmins of 'outcaste' groups, once called 'Untouchables'. This pejorative label Gandhi replaced with Harijans, 'Children of God'. Included in this low-status category are sweepers, washermen, leather-workers, basket-makers, potters and weavers – that is, anyone affiliated to Harijan castes, whatever their actual occupation. Harijan castes are also ranked hierarchically among themselves.

Despite vigorous efforts by many individuals and organisations, locally and nationally, including governments, to improve the conditions and prospects of these Harijans, traditional caste feeling is slow to change, and its burden falls heavily upon them. Nevertheless, in some respects substantial progress has been made, especially where groups of Harijans organise their own advancement, for instance by forming co-operative units for production or marketing. The widening experience of the Harijans and others stimulates modifications of caste attitudes, while industrial development undermines the interlocking set of complementary occupations which forms the economic aspect of the caste system.

One reason why the stigma of caste remains a powerful factor in rural life is the thoroughness with which the sense of caste identity and exclusiveness is transmitted from one generation to the next. This is done not only by explicit teaching of young children but also through unconsciously transmitted structures in language, posture, gesture and the physical system of village, house and domestic material culture. That caste relations are reflected physically is no accident but directly connected with the concept of ritual pollution.

By sexual abstinence and other forms of self-control the 'ideal' Hindu male seeks to conserve spiritual strength and purity as a kind of seminal (the word is appropriate) essence. This originates in food which the body converts first to

This baby, suspended safely in a traditional turned-wood cradle, acquires cultural values from her physical environment as well as by deliberate instruction.

A purpose-built workshop, rented from another, wealthier weaver. The door and window admit light so the weaver can work longer hours. The electric light is weak and often unreliable. The floor is of mud and cow-dung, finished in a pattern of regular curves.

blood and finally to semen which is believed to be stored in the head. Two main consequences follow: first, any exudation from the body is regarded as a negation of retained purity. Faeces, semen and saliva are all dangerous in these terms because of their symbolic opposition to spiritual strength. Saliva is particularly dangerous because it emanates from the head itself, and for this reason is thought of as 'spoiled' semen. Second, as food is the physical origin of spiritual purity, any direct physical or indirect spiritual contamination of food or drink before it is taken into the body is dangerous to spiritual well-being.

In the village such activities as sex, washing, cleaning pots, urination, defecation, food preparation and eating are therefore subject to careful precautions against the risk of ritual pollution. These precautions have become part of the structure of daily life and are thought of in exactly the same terms as any other practical task. It can now be seen how caste operates simultaneously on social, economic and ideological levels: castes are occupational groups; relations between them involve asymmetric exchanges of goods and services; and such relations are ordered by the concept of ritual pollution. It should also be clear how such a complex inhibits change. The idea of ritual pollution and the relationship between the physical and spiritual is contained deep in the routines of daily activities, including the physical means and conditions which are created for carrying them out. This ensures a thorough transmission of traditional caste values, independent of conscious intention.

The most obvious physical expression of caste differentiation in a village is the distribution of the different khadki compounds between the various caste communities and the arrangement of wells and tank; but there are subtler adaptations, too, which can be seen in the house. As well as by precautions against ritual pollution from outside the caste, domestic life is circumscribed by rules governing relations between members of the same joint family, with particular importance attached to relations between men and women and between young and old.

The house

Most houses in Vasna are modest; the most elaborate, with two or very occasionally three storeys, brick-built and stone-floored, belong to the local Rajputs or Patels. The weavers' houses are of a mixture of mud and cow-dung plaster over rough brick or wickerwork walls. Roofs are of red earthenware tiles, half cylinders, supported by squared timbers and bamboo. The floors are only rarely flagged; usually they are constructed of cow-dung like the walls. Often the floor surface is finished in a pattern of repeated curved or zigzag ridges.

It is a house's internal elaboration rather than its overall size which best indicates the relative wealth of the owner. Space is simply not available for enlarging the house beyond the original plot if the owner's wealth increases. Social as well as physical constraints are involved: in general a relatively better-off member of any local caste community will tend to avoid advertising this fact; he will otherwise be subject to levelling claims or to resentment if these are not met. In traditional terms to display one's relative affluence was to attract thieves. Any extra money may therefore go towards an occasional luxury such as a radio set, but larger sums are disposed of outside the domestic household.

Internal features of a house mainly reflect shared social values about boundaries, ritual pollution and the proper realms and roles of men and women, family members and outsiders. In the weaver's house the general association of the back room with women's work and the hearth, while the front room is the weaver's workshop, has already been mentioned. The adaptation of this arrangement according to practical circumstances emphasises that it is the functional rather than the structural aspect that is important. In other words, the allocation of space has to ensure the convenient pursuit of household occupations, and departures from traditional patterns are permitted where appropriate. The necessary rules of social life are, in any case, always accommodated. Not even the hearth is certain to be found in any one fixed position; sometimes a portable *chula* is used outside, but cooking, which is exclusively women's work, is always done away from the door, by a side wall or in a corner, to minimise interference with, and the risk of pollution from, other people and activities.

This functional flexibility may be partly an expression of traditional poverty. It has recently been suggested that the practical interaction which is necessary between members of the same family, together with the double exclusion of outsiders from the caste khadki and the individual dwelling, allows the physical expression of social barriers to be relaxed to the level of gestures, even when

Above A street scene in Dholka, a small town. Some wage-earning weavers operate power looms here in modest workshops.

Right Part of the ornate façade of a 17th-century traditional house in Ahmedabad city. Many structural features are reminiscent of more modest village prototypes.

a family's wealth would allow the elaboration of interior structures. This interpretation is supported by the fact that in urban houses, which are more vulnerable to visits from outsiders, permanent partitions and fixed arrangements or furnishings are more in evidence.

After the khadki house has been constructed, and as the owner's fortunes permit, a series of alterations will be made to the original simple shell structure. First a loft is added to the rear portion of the house; this is a typical feature of most houses in Vasna today. Its function is mainly as a fuel store, but other items are kept there too. Clearly such an addition makes sense because of the limited floor space available. In houses more typical of the classic north Gujarat khadki, in which the rear part of the ground floor is reserved for women's activities, a ventilator is added to the rear wall, in the form of a barred window, to allow the escape of smoke from the hearth. Where the hearth is in the front room this alteration is unnecessary, but with the weaver in the rear of the house a window for extra light and a door for access are necessary anyway.

The loft is supported on a transverse beam which runs parallel to the dividing line between the front and rear rooms of the house. The next stage in the elaboration of the house's interior is to build a partition wall so that the whole of the rear part of the house becomes an enclosed area. Access from the front is provided by means of a door. In the typical khadki house this now becomes a fully lockable strong-room; except via the internal partition door, there is no access. Where the rear wall is provided with a door, as in the majority of weavers' houses in Vasna, the whole security function of the rear room is undermined, unless the back door can be locked securely. In practice the most elaborate and strongest door in the house is the front door, although the internal partition door may also be stoutly made. As a rule, the door in the rear wall is weaker than either of these, but this may simply reflect the lesser importance of security nowadays. This safe rear room is called the *ordo*, and the

Above A weaver's wife and son in a room used mainly for storage.

Right The security of the traditional ordo, the back room especially associated with women, was assured by a strong internal door such as this one. Pegs, hooks, shelves and niches allow storage where there is limited floor space.

Above Large grain-storage jars (kothis) in the corner of the ordo in a weaver's house.

Above Part of the ordo used for storing water-pots and containers for keeping or serving food.
Opposite Walls beside and above a front door are sometimes painted with simple designs.

orthodox use of it is therefore for the storage of valuables. The front room is called the *parsal*, and the veranda, which many houses have, is the *otlo*.

The house of a relatively wealthy villager could in theory be provided with a full loft, which would become, in due course, a proper second storey. This is a development which happens only relatively rarely because of the technical difficulty of achieving adequate height at first-floor level. The two-storey building is thus normally planned as such from the beginning and is characteristic of the family whose relative wealth is long-established; the adaptation of an existing single-storey house is impractical, however much the owner's fortunes may have risen.

Nevertheless, the arrangement of the upper floor in a purpose-built two-storey house of the kind seen not only in Ahmedabad but also in towns, or larger villages like Vasna, and the position and inclination of the stairs follow that of the half-loft single-storey structure. The stairs are in the same position and of the same steepness, and even of a closely similar construction, as the ladder which gives access to the loft in a single-storey house. Like the loft, the upper storey is a zone accorded relatively low status, to be occupied by younger members of the family or by married sons. It may be that this lower status is reflected in the fact that the exterior woodcarving is usually less elaborate on the upper façade of a two-storey house than on its lower façade; but a simpler explanation may be that less carving can be seen there than at ground level.

The ridge of the house, its highest part, is always situated nearer to the rear than to the front of the plot of land which the house occupies. There is no apparent structural reason why this should be so, but the motive may have been simply to locate the (structurally) important ridge over the (socially) important ordo, which contained valuables and the hearth; this may be so, but even more important from a practical perspective is the correlation which this arrangement achieves between the highest part of the roof and the position of the hearth from which smoke rises to escape from the house.

It remains to give further details of how the component parts of the individual khadki house are used from day to day. First, the veranda or otlo: this is the zone occupied during the day and night by men, when they are not in the fields or their workshops, or when colder weather does not force them indoors. It is also the place where men visitors are received and business discussed. Women may also perform chores in the same area but only when this will not interfere with its other, male-orientated functions. It is, of course, often necessary for the women to wash pots on the veranda so that the waste water can flow away from the house into the subterranean soak-pit. The otlo is also the place where all members of the household clean their teeth in the early morning using a nim (neem) twig for the purpose, and taking perhaps as long as twenty minutes to do so. This period is simultaneously used for informal gossip between neighbours. Individuals may wander over to neighbours' verandas or mingle in the khadki yard. In wet weather some of the men's activities normally conducted here are transferred to the front room, the parsal.

The parsal, the front room, is the *de facto* zone for women's work while the men are out in the fields or working elsewhere. It is here that the household's water supply is kept and most of the cooking done. It is an area rarely entered by strangers, but less confined and smoke-filled than the rear room when this is used for cooking. Although it retains a multi-purpose character, the parsal is mainly used by women when other factors permit. This always put a premium on space, to which one adaptation was the development of such storage aids as shelves, niches, hooks and pegs. Significantly it is here, where special visitors might be received, that objects from which prestige may derive, such as religious prints, photographic portraits of relatives of higher status, and a corpus of brassware, are conspicuously displayed.

Used with cotton quilts, the strong cot (charpoy) is a comfortable couch generally reserved for men's use.

The back room, the ordo, is the locus of the hearth in the classic arrangement. Here the cooking was done, usually near the partition wall, while the *kothi* grain-containers were from preference lined up against the rear wall or in one corner. But in Vasna, in addition to such adaptations of these internal arrangements which have been prompted by the needs of the weaver, many housewives do most cooking in the parsal, regardless of how the ordo is used. Traditionally the ordo is the women's special area. The normal use of this room for the storage of valuables may therefore have deterred the potential (male) thief to an appreciable extent, since its allocation to women ensured for it an aura of danger through the possibility of ritual pollution by association with menstruation or childbirth.

Domestic equipment

Members of a weaver's family in Vasna use a narrow range of household apparatus of clearly defined types: furniture for sitting and sleeping or for storage; containers of various kinds for liquids, food and other perishables; equipment for preparing food, cooking and lighting; a mirror, devotional prints or figures, and mementoes such as photographs; various papers and notebooks; (often) a radio; spare clothing; quilts and other cloths and bedding; sometimes an old turned-wood baby's cradle which can be dismantled for storage; a supply of cow-dung, dried in flat cakes for fuel; a variety of equipment connected with weaving or spinning or winding yarn; and perhaps a European-style chair and table.

A charpoy is multi-functional. It can be used as a bed or as a drying frame for clothes.

The main item of furniture is the multi-purpose cot (*charpoy*, *khatco*), a four-legged wooden frame bearing a patterned interlacing of thick string. There are several of these in every house. As the string stretches with use, it is tautened by taking up the slack at one end. For this purpose a space is left at one end of the cot to which the adjacent edge of the string covering is attached by long, adjustable loops of the same or different material. The cot serves mainly as a bed or couch, used in conjunction with quilts or blankets; or outside as a storage bench, or on its side as a drying frame, wind-break or even sunshade. When out of use, it can be stored on its side or end against a wall. It is in this position that the patterned interlacing can best be seen. In Vasna this is usually a diagonal design or rectangles diminishing into the centre.

The most highly valued piece of furniture in the house is probably the iron-bound wooden storage chest (two types – *patara* or *majuh*), usually provided with one or two pairs of small wooden wheels which only in theory allow it to be moved around inside the house; in practice, it never is. The chest is very heavy, padlocked, and the sheet-iron mountings usually bear punched or stamped geometrical designs. In such secure containers are kept jewellery and costumes.

Many features of local life reflect the importance of security against theft, and the general lack of ostentation can also be interpreted in these terms. The risk of theft is perhaps less now than in the past, but precautions have become incorporated into the traditional culture. Doors are thus typically reinforced with stout cross timbers fixed in position with iron nails or rivets, while windows and ventilators are fitted with strong iron grilles or in poorer houses with less elaborate wooden ones. The sheer size of storage chests ensures that they can accommodate bulky items like costumes, but they are made heavy enough to deter unauthorised removal. A full chest will not normally leave the house unless for the payment of a dowry, and even with its wheels requires the co-operation of several people to move it. The great brass *katodan* dowry-container, used by some communities in Gujarat but not in Vasna, also works on the same principle of practical immobility. So does the kothi, the large earthenware grain-container found in pairs or threes in the back room of most houses in rural Gujarat, including Vasna.

Food is stored in a variety of containers. Ghee (clarified butter), which traditionally and especially among nomadic groups was kept in portable wooden flasks, is today found in tins; likewise spices, although sometimes an older, specialised set of wooden spice-receptacles may be found in use. The storage of grain is a different matter: while nowadays some may be kept in sheet-steel trunks, the bulk of the family's supply is retained in large kothi jars. The use of other containers, or simply piling rice on the floor of an unoccupied room, suggests only temporary storage of a surplus prior to its sale.

The kothi may be as much as 1·5 m high and 1 m in diameter. It is usually too wide ever to be removed from the storage room, which is usually at the back of the house, the same room as that used for cooking. It follows that when the back room is used for weaving, so that the space allocated to men and women switches from the classic pattern, the kothi jars remain where they originated, in a corner or against a wall. Another consequence of their size is that the jars cannot be replaced with others of the same size if they are broken, but are instead repaired by filling holes or cracks with fresh clay and sometimes by supporting the entire structure with cord bindings if there is a risk of their collapsing.

The position, size and patched character of these jars all indicate the great importance of a grain store for a family's welfare and security. When the house is first built, the jars are brought in and set in position. When internal walls are added later, the doorway need not be large enough to allow the jars through for there are no circumstances in which these will need to be shifted. Large jars clearly reflect the prestige, or at least the satisfaction, which attaches to an ample food supply; but they are also very practical containers. The kothi has a relatively small, flat base or a slightly rounded one, so the jar is supported by packing with clay around the outside to a few centimetres above the floor. This takes up a small part of the limited floor space available, but more importantly it exposes a minimum of surface area to damage from the floor, such as rodent attack. The jar bulges in the middle, which makes the contents virtually inaccessible to ambitious, climbing rodents and improves the efficiency of the container in terms of the ratio of capacity to surface area.

The large size of the kothi, suggesting the importance of the family's grain supply, simultaneously reflects the traditional risk and common experience of famine, which in this part of India has always been serious. A large jar is necessary not only if an adequate surplus is to be held against future shortage but also as a precaution against theft from outside.

In addition to the wooden storage chest and the cot most houses contain other, smaller items of furniture such as two- or four-legged wooden supports, positioned against a wall, for water vessels; often these are fitted with decorative elements such as carvings in the form of stylised horses' heads. Wall-shelves of a similar form are used for storing smaller, lighter vessels, crockery and beakers. China cups may be slung from these on hooks. Some households have cupboards of various kinds, but traditional wall-pegs and suspension hooks are still widely used for lighter objects like clothes or small containers. These devices are well suited to the design of houses whose floor space is limited and where storage is largely a battle against vermin.

Often quilts and other textiles are stored on a special rack (*damachia*), which may be kept in the same multi-purpose room as the great kothi jars and lockable chests and trunks. Whether on such a rack or on a storage chest, textiles of varied colours and patterns are laid one on top of the other, the larger and thicker at the bottom, and the whole pile is typically secured by string to prevent collapse. This way of storing things is paralleled by the method adopted for metal and other vessels on shelves or benches, where larger items support others in columns which therefore taper towards the smaller ones at the top. In some parts of Gujarat this feature is termed *mand*, but it is familar throughout the state and elsewhere in India. Women fetching water in brass vessels often stack them efficiently in twos or threes on their heads, and pots stacked on the ground to dry or on a cart for transport have the same appearance. Clearly such a mode of stacking or storage is presupposed in the graded series of vessels and other items which families use, and probably has something to do with allowing the use of a large number of vessels by people occupying a limited space. If so, then it reflects not only the limitation on space in traditional houses but also social rules governing eating and cooking.

A lot of containers are needed, of course, where a family depends on its women frequently fetching water from a well or other source which may be inconveniently far from the house, and where strict rules, connected with the risk of ritual pollution, must be observed in the preparation and consumption of food. A shining array of brass, copper, or stainless-steel containers is also a source of prestige for most housewives and attractively reflects not only the flickering light of the fire in the hearth but also the family's prosperity.

Apart from the kothi, ceramic vessels in regular household use include water-storage pots of various kinds (*goro* or *golo*, *ghado*, *kundi*); smaller pots with narrower necks (*bampli*, *matlu*), used, when a metal vessel is not, for fetching water or otherwise for cooking; a shallow dish (*kaledu*) for making chapatis; small dish-shaped covers (*dhakan*, *dhankan*) for the mouths of pots; and saucer-shaped black earthenware eating dishes (*vatku*), as well as small lamps. Nowadays patterned and glazed china cups and saucers are often used for drinking tea (*char*).

The place of many of these vessels is now being usurped by lighter, more durable and easier-to-clean metal containers and dishes. This process of switching from ceramics to metal probably began in the late nineteenth century because the transfer of the Gujarati term *thobalun*, for a shallow earthenware eating dish with a raised rim, to a brass version of the same thing is recorded for this period. What has happened is that metal vessels have now become accessible to many families; a few decades ago, although most people had small brass drinking cups (*loti*) for personal use, only better-off families had brassware in any quantity.

The substitution now in progress takes a practical course. In some houses a small amount of grain is kept in metal trunks but most is stored in efficient kothi jars; likewise drinking water is now commonly fetched in brass, steel or aluminium vessels carried on the head, but it can still be kept cooler at home in a semi-porous earthenware pot. For flatter items like dishes, plates and covers for pots, in which the risk of breakage is increased by frequent use, metal is much more durable than earthenware and not very expensive.

Brass or copper vessels are especially necessary for large-scale catering at religious festivals or family or caste gatherings. In the nineteenth century sets of vessels were sometimes bought co-operatively by members of the poorer castes to be kept by an agreed nominee until required for a special occasion. This use of metal vessels ties in with anti-pollution rules which forbid the use of the same piece of earthenware for eating by different people. A vessel made of a mixture of brass and copper is especially favoured, but any metal article is regarded as inherently less liable to ritual pollution than one made of earthenware. The prestige attaching to a set of metal pots and pans therefore derives from a deeper source than the association of such vessels with the better-off members of the community; they are also spiritually desirable. Copper–brass vessels have been called *Ganga-Jamni*, signifying the auspicious confluence of the holy Rivers Ganges and Jumna at Allahabad. This underlines the inherent symbolic purity of these two metals in combination, but the same general attitude also carries over to some extent to aluminium and stainless steel, neither of which, of course, tarnishes in normal use.

The standard large brass water-carrying vessel bears the same name, ghado, as its earthenware prototype. The loti is a beaker for drinking water, the larger *degdo* for water storage. There are a variety of bowls, dishes and trays in which food is served and from which it is eaten: vatko, *tranhali* and *thali.* Versions of pottery forms generally retain their original names, which therefore appear to refer to function rather than to material. For example, *kathrot* is a bowl for mixing dough for bread (*rotla*) whether of earthenware or brass. However, the earthenware lamp (*kodiyu*) becomes *divo* in brass or stainless steel.

The substitution of metal for earthenware also highlights another aspect of traditional culture. Cooking is a process which not only renders food more palatable; it also has the effect of ritually purifying it. The application of fire likewise purifies earthenware itself: this is why the clay which the potter works into the desired shape is regarded as ritually impure, while the fired vessel which he later produces is acceptable for use. Cooking vessels are still often made of earthenware, while those used for the serving and eating of food are more rapidly being substituted with metal ones: the hearth purifies the cooking-pot.

Household utensils made of other materials are few but significant. The

wooden mortar (*khodaniyu*) and pestle (*sambelu*) are used for grinding spices and grain, though often the latter is taken for grinding to a local mill. *Supdu* is the basketry winnowing-fan, which is still common throughout the village even though other devices could serve better or as well. For instance, in other parts of Gujarat the same functions are performed by means of an adapted shovel-blade made of metal. This has the advantage that it is easily cleaned, and being metal it may be favoured for symbolic reasons. However, the retention of the basketry version in Vasna probably reflects the social commitment to patronise the few local basket-makers, the bhangis, who otherwise would have few economic prospects. Apart from its use in winnowing, the supdu is often used to encourage a fire in place of bellows.

Inside the house an important element which has not yet been replaced by the now universal electric light (using bulbs with very low wattage) is the lamp and the lampstand (*samai*). One reason for this is that the electricity supply tends to be erratic; many households keep a hurricane lamp and traditional oil-lamps for use on special occasions like rituals or festivals, or when the mains fail. The electric battery torch is nowadays increasingly used, especially when it is necessary to move about the village at night.

With regard to the importance of avoiding ritual pollution, an indispensable utensil is the ubiquitous, short-lived and disposable broom, made out of a bunch of straw or grass tied at one end and tapered at the other with the central stalks left longer than those outside. Because of its associations the broom is stored out of the way.

The accoutrements of most households are therefore generally unelaborate and functional. This is partly related to cost and partly to limitations on space. Equipment is often multi-purpose where this is not proscribed by religious considerations. Decoration of utilitarian equipment is usually restrained. However, this by no means indicates a narrowly functional attitude towards their use. On the contrary, the objects themselves, like the space in which they are used, are highly charged with religious significance.

Household items with a special or explicit religious significance include coloured devotional prints, framed or in the form of calendars advertising commercial companies; and small three-dimensional images of deities, of which one of the most popular among weavers is the elephant-god, Ganesh. A *toran*, of appliqué, embroidery or beadwork – or all three – may be hung above the door, especially on important occasions, while a square of similarly decorative appearance (*chakla*), often bearing mirror-work, may be hung on an inside wall. In Vasna, however, neither the toran nor chakla is as common today as in western Gujarat, although they appear to be part of the local tradition. These decorations incorporate religious motifs and are held to be auspicious, but they come closer than anything else in the house to a flourish of decoration for its own sake.

The avowed purpose of the toran is to welcome visitors, a message which is often reinforced with the English word 'Welcome', usually in the characteristic form 'Wel-come' or 'Wel Come', painted on the outside wall to one side of the door. Welcoming the guest, the auspicious visitor, is logically not equivalent to warding off danger, which appears to be a residual function of the toran. The front door is the point where the intrusion of malevolent spirits has to be prevented for the welfare of the household. In the past leaves were thought to ward off evil, and mango leaves, in particular, are still used for this purpose, applied to the door-frame. All the carvings found on Gujarati door-frames are decorated with leaves as the dominant motif, and the ultra-auspicious Ganesh often occupies a central position in carved lintels. The cloth toran also strikingly resembles leaves, and the string of spent electric light-bulbs, which can occasionally be seen suspended above a window, may be a modern version of the same thing.

Using a special knife, a basket-maker splits a length of bamboo. His water-pipe rests against the wall behind.

A young housewife from a relatively well-off village family, rocking her baby in a cradle. The welcoming/ protective toran above the door is surrounded by religious prints and photographs of relatives.

Spent light-bulbs strung across a barred window create a novel decorative effect and may imitate the protective function of the traditional toran.

Food

Like most Gujaratis, the inhabitants of Vasna are vegetarian. Ordinary cultivators and craftsmen and their families eat simply and reasonably well. The main staple is brown rice eaten boiled with fried vegetables and flat chapatis (*rotli*) made of wheat flour. The rice and vegetables are often cooked together as *khichadi*. An important source of protein is pulses, such as *mung* and gram, usually fried in ground-nut oil or, for special occasions, in ghee. Food is moderately spiced, mainly with chillies and garlic; turmeric, mustard and fenugreek (*methi*) are also used. Onions and potatoes are popular, fried with other vegetables, but onions are also eaten raw as an accompaniment to the cooked food.

Water is usually drunk with the meal and is used afterwards to wash out the mouth and to clean the fingers of the right hand which have been used to transfer the food in small quantities to the mouth. The left hand is regarded as ritually impure and is never used in connection with the mouth. A little ghee, trickled on to an otherwise dryish mound of rice, makes it not only more palatable but also easier to form into small lumps. Ghee is a prestige food, strongly associated with ritual purity through its derivation from milk, and generally is used only sparingly. As an exceptional treat, a dessert dish is concocted of wheat flour and sugar, which is eaten with perhaps a drink of curds and some fresh fruit. The main meal may occasionally be enlivened with pickled mangoes, lemons or limes. Very occasionally, hens' eggs are eaten too.

People are generally pragmatic about mealtimes. If it is necessary to leave the house early for the fields, a substantial meal will be eaten at daybreak or earlier, and perhaps another will be eaten in late afternoon. Mealtimes follow the pattern of work. A morning meal usually derives from food cooked the previous evening. A light snack differs less in kind than in amount from the two main meals on which the majority of villagers subsist. The chief intake between these two standard meals is of tea, drunk hot and sweet, the milk boiled together with the water and leaves.

Meals are taken near to the hearth, that is, in the zone normally reserved for women's activities. The logic of this is clear: since the position of the hearth is designed to avoid the risk of ritual pollution during cooking, eating might as well also take place in the same area. Invariably, men eat before the women.

Kitchen refuse is deposited outside the khadki into a pond reserved for this purpose. Formerly, when cow-dung was used for manure rather than fuel, each family had its own dunghill to which household rubbish would be added. Although the communal rubbish-pond can also be used as a source of fertiliser when it dries up in the hot weather, this is not done in Vasna as it is elsewhere.

Except for snacks taken in the fields, all meals are eaten from metal or earthenware dishes on the floor. This reflects partly the comfort of sitting cross-legged in the accustomed manner, and partly the pattern of serving the food in a variety of containers scattered about; but above all it reflects the ritual purity of the floor in the vicinity of the hearth: a reminder that due precautions have been taken during cooking and food preparation generally. This is to a certain extent a matter of cleaning, but it is also to do with the material of which the floor is made.

Cow-dung is a convenient material with which to coat the earthen floor and is used for this purpose throughout India. However, in a society which attaches special ritual importance to both cows and dung it is obvious that symbolic factors are influential here. One attractive argument runs as follows: the floor, as the locus of both sexual activity and childbirth, is passively associated with fertility; cow-dung, as an agricultural fertiliser, helps to increase crops and is thus strongly associated with the general idea of fertility; the application of cow-dung to the floor thus symbolically encourages the

Blankets made of wool and goathair have an even more restricted market than cotton pachedis, being worn only by certain herdsmen and lasting longer. Here a weaver in a village not far from Sanand town applies starch to woollen warp threads to prepare them for weaving.

A weaver holding the wool/goathair wrap or blanket (*dhabalo*) which he has made.

fertility and prosperity of the household. Possibly it is this direct link between cow-dung and fertility which, carried over to the source of the dung, accounts for the cow's sacred and revered status in India. However, this hypothesis is probably an over-simplification, and whatever the best explanation of the various associations involved, it is only necessary to note their existence in order to make sense of what villagers do. The cow, being a symbol of purity, produces excrement with the opposite of the usual connotations of excrement for Hindus. There seems to be a general effort to associate the house with such material, for not only the floor but also the walls are made, or partly made, of cow-dung, and the use of the same material as fuel, even though this has come about only because of the unavailability of firewood, adds to the pervasiveness of symbolic purity in the domestic context.

Dress

In Vasna the standard dress for men consists of a tailored half-sleeved or sleeveless cotton vest (*banian*) and an untailored cotton loincloth (*dhoti* or *pachedi*), both normally, or nominally, white. Few men wear head-gear, but the Gandhi cap is favoured by some older men. Footwear is usually non-traditional; a wide variety of styles are worn, either copied by local shoemakers in near-by towns or villages, or bought from shops in the town or city. Feet are bare indoors, but in most outdoor contexts sandals (*chappals*) are worn. In colder weather, and in the early morning or late evening, both men and women will use a simple woollen blanket wrap.

Two groups are conspicuous exceptions to this pattern of dress. First, the men of the herding communities, Bharvads or Rabaris, maintain their own distinctive traditions. The dhoti is then a coarse cotton pachedi with strikingly coloured borders of red, black, green or other colours, with additional patterns. A pachedi of similar type is also worn as a loose wrap over the upper half of the body, but beneath this a Bharvad will wear a tight-fitting, long-sleeved white shirt which stops at the waist; its place is taken among Rabari men by a similar garment characterised by vertical gathers which flare from just below the chest. Both groups invariably wear turbans or loosely wrapped lengths of red or white cotton cloth. The shoes are also traditional, pointed at the toe, high at the back with a thick, multi-layered leather sole and heel. This feature, at least, seems to protect the feet from thorns or sharp stones in the rough areas where the animals graze. These traditionalists are also more particular about the kind of cold-weather wrap they wear, favouring a wool/goathair mixture with practical, waterproof qualities and distinctive designs.

The second group which departs from normal dress consists of younger men and those with above-average education or familiarity with city life. Not all of these have adopted city ways, and their presence in the village indicates that none has abandoned tradition comprehensively; but their dress suggests an unmistakable orientation. It is very unlikely that these young men will ever in later life wear a dhoti or banian, although the blanket wrap is common among them, and its practicality for occasional use probably guarantees its future. They wear polyester or cotton shirts, often with patterns, and casual slacks, while their shoes will often be more elaborate than those worn by their elders. No one, of course, wears socks.

This city-orientated group has no counterpart among the women of the village, although most, except the old and some members of the herding communities, will wear clothes made of synthetic or other material bought or originating in the city. The styles remain traditional, however. Two main types of costume are found: more traditional but less common is the combination of a short-sleeved close-fitting banian which stops short just below the breasts, beneath an adjustable loose wrap which can cover the head, and a wide skirt (*ghagra*), tied at the waist. The other style, which is probably increasing in popularity, is the standard sari. Women go barefoot more often than men but also wear kinds of light sandals or shoes when the occasion demands. Except for the old, including widows, who wear very dark colours or black, most women combine vivid colours and patterns in striking contrast to the usually unostentatious dress of men.

To this, women add a profusion of jewellery, most of it cheap and colourful, in the form of anklets, bangles, necklaces and rings on fingers and in the nose and ears. Among the men only the herders wear jewellery: gold earrings are part of traditional attire. Their womenfolk do not dress very differently from other village women, except that they are, if anything, even more resplendently attired and more traditional in their tastes. It is certainly the case, borne out by comparisons elsewhere in Gujarat, that this contrast between the colourfulness of men and women's dress is a thoroughly traditional feature.

Festivals and fairs

Economic and religious activities are often combined in regular gatherings which attract hundreds or thousands of villagers and townsfolk. In Gujarat most fairs are localised in temple towns or other places of pilgrimage where worship and trading are both intensive. The majority of fairs coincide with significant days in the Hindu calendar, but the festivals of Muslims and Jains

are also often combined with fairs. Many fairs are attended by members of all religious communities.

One of these, the biggest fair in Ahmedabad District and usually drawing villagers from neighbouring districts too, is held at Vautha, not far from Dholka. Up to 200,000 people gather for two or three days in November on the flat dusty plain of the Sabarmati where it meets the River Vatrak. The Sabarmati has been considered holy for thousands of years, and its place in the history and thought of Gujarat was given further symbolic meaning when Gandhi founded his first ashram on its banks to the north of Ahmedabad.

In the vicinity there is an auspicious confluence of seven important rivers, and Dholka itself, only thirteen kilometres distant, is believed to be the place where the Pandava brothers of the classical Hindu epic, the *Mahabharata*, spent the last year of their exile in disguise. Vautha is also significant as the site of austerities which were effected by Kartik Swami or Kartikeya, son of Siva; his footprints are worshipped there by devotees.

Since shortly after Independence Vautha fair has been organised by the local authorities and has become more formal than it once was. It very size and its popularity among different sections of the population have encouraged the national and local administration to use it as an opportunity for mass education on such topics as farming and contraception.

The mass encampment at Vautha fair. Most families erect awnings over their bullock carts and stay for several days.

All this is an extension of the autonomous and traditional character of the event. The majority of participants are villagers, from all castes, including Harijans. Food sold at the fair includes wheat, bajri, rice, vegetables, sugar and fruit, while sweets and other items are also sold for immediate consumption. There is also a bazaar of thousands of donkeys brought by Vanjara traders from outside the district, and of a smaller number of camels. The donkeys, in particular, are strikingly decorated (and identified) with bright pink and other colours on their necks and backs; most of them are sold to contractors for the transport of building materials.

It is not only religion or routine economics that brings villagers to Vautha; they come, above all, for the social contact and entertainment that it offers, and for the opportunity to buy rare or novelty items that are normally unavailable in their home villages. A thousand or more hawkers sell a huge variety of articles. Traditional jugglers, magicians, musicians, dancers and acrobats vie with modern fairground amusements like Ferris wheels for the attention of the visitor. It is still a genuine folk-gathering or *lokmela*.

Accommodation at Vautha fair reflects its folk character. Those who have travelled for a day or more bring tents, and thousands set up camp in and around the bullock carts in which they have ridden, draping an awning against the sun and cooking on an impromptu hearth. The advantage of this means of transport, and of conveniently portable domestic necessities, is obvious in such circumstances. Without the carts the whole social and economic character of the fair would be different. Not only would fewer people attend, but they would come from less far away and would not need to stay so long, or be unable to, unless accommodation and catering were provided. The opportunity for social contact would be reduced and with it everyone's enjoyment. The purchase of goods beyond what people could immediately use or carry themselves would decline, so the content of trade would suffer. In these ways the fair is dependent for its present form on the continued use of the bullock cart. It is unlikely that trucks or lorries, which are increasingly used, despite higher initial purchase and running costs, could be used as traditional carts are, to convey whole families to and from the fair over long distances with all their necessary household equipment.

As well as promoting social and economic interaction, festivals also reinforce social and religious values. These roles are interrelated: at the economic level the fair-festival is a supra-local clearing-house for material goods and services; socially it establishes or strengthens solidarity within castes and dependence between them on a wider scale than usual; at the symbolic level the festival ties individual and group experience to the cosmic order, advertising and celebrating the close connection to ordinary living of the deities and events on which the festival focuses, and which express Hindu values.

Some more general festivals which are celebrated all over India, such as Holi and Diwali, have no particular local focus, so do not involve the kind of intensive contact which forms the basis for trade. One annual festival of this kind which is especially popular in Gujarat is Makar Sankranti, celebrated on 14 January, a public holiday. On this day millions of brightly coloured paper kites are flown on strings made sharp with powdered glass. The festival is the high point of a long period of weeks or months of competitive kite-flying in which the winner cuts his opponent's string with his own. All India Radio broadcasts commentaries on organised kite-flying competitions. On the night of Makar Sankranti thousands of kites, to which are attached paper lanterns enclosing lighted candles, are released into the sky. The most spectacular effect, and the worst fire damage, is restricted to the towns and cities (especially Ahmedabad), but the festival is also observed in the countryside, and kites can be bought at almost any time of the year from village shops as well as stalls in city streets.

Paper kites displayed for sale outside a village shop. To the left is a post-box. Kite flying is most intensive on the festival of Makar Sankranti, but boys practise for months beforehand.

Makar Sankranti is *Uttarayana*, a Hindu harvest festival coinciding with the winter solstice when the sun is regarded as starting its northward journey. It is the time when deities awake from a long period of inactivity. This gives the festival its theme of ritual renewal, in which offerings of food and special diet play a specially important part. People are enjoined to give alms, usually food, to Brahmins and to acquire religious merit generally.

At this time some people follow scriptural advice and eat oily foods which are believed to ensure vitality. Cows are also worshipped and given boiled cereals; deities in temples dedicated to Vishnu are also presented with grain-derived delicacies. All this relates to the fact that the monsoon crop has been harvested; and the festival highlights the relation between ritual and economic activity, which are symbolically fused in food. The kites especially focus attention on the sky and thus probably symbolise the solar movement which is ostensibly celebrated.

Bullock carts

It has already been pointed out that the bullock cart makes an important contribution to fairs like that at Vautha; but its main role is as a working vehicle in a farming context. There are about a hundred bullock carts in Vasna, and twice as many bicycles. These are by far the most important local means of transport under the control of the villagers themselves. In addition, the local bus service is cheap, regular, reliable and accessible on the National Highway a

81

couple of kilometres from the village itself. There is also a fairly accessible rail service near by. By these means villagers can easily reach the towns of Bavla or Dholka, or Ahmedabad city. The village boasts one motor car and two motor cycles, all owned by Rajputs. There are only two camel carts and two tractors.

It is estimated that a traditional bullock cart (*gadu*) will last between three to four generations. This is a remarkable tribute to the sturdiness of its design and construction. Most of the carts are now of a somewhat smaller modern type (*galedi*) with pneumatic rubber tyres on truck-type wheels, and various structural simplifications. For example, the curved wooden axle-supports on the outside of the wheels are now hardly ever seen, even where the cart is generally traditional in other respects, with metal tyres and spoked wooden wheels. An important reason for this change is that the traditional cart costs about twice as much as the modern version, which being lighter is easier to manoeuvre.

The traditional cart is two-wheeled and drawn by a pair of bullocks. The yoke is tied to the shaft with a more or less elaborately patterned lashing of coir or other rope. The junction of these two elements is treated as important, and to be effective obviously needs the optimum combination of firmness and flexibility. Both the shaft, consisting of several divergent timbers, and the floor, sides and ends of the box unit are reinforced with sparingly decorated bands of iron and brass. The rough terrain in which the cart is used in narrow rutted tracks between the fields and the heavy loads carried demand a careful arrangement to preserve the main load-bearing components – the axle and the wheels. This is achieved by means of wooden axle-supports and other elements which help to spread the burden.

Along the shaft there is often a double row of holes into which stout poles can be inserted to provide extra loading space for fodder, and in the floor of the cart other poles can be erected as supports for an awning to shelter passengers or protect the load. The cart can thus easily convert into a temporary mobile home when longer journeys need to be made.

Pot making

There are only a few members of the potters' caste in Vasna, most of them cultivators. Only two or three families still make pots, and their future looks uncertain. What they make is a response to contemporary pressures on their craft. It is uneconomic to create pots for which metal containers are an increasingly popular alternative, but there are two types which are withstanding competition: the standard, unglazed red earthenware water-pot (*matka*), which keeps water cooler than any metal vessel can; and the larger black or grey earthenware storage jar (*kothi*) for grain or water. This type of kothi is smaller, of darker clay, and has a different shape from the type found in most houses. Although smaller, it is cheaper than a metal container with the same capacity, and it is unlikely to be significantly less durable since it is normally used in a fixed position in the house.

Clay is dug locally and larger impurities are carefully removed before it is mixed in a pit by treading with water and with bajri chaff as a filler. When a water-pot is to be made, the heavy, clay-encrusted, rim-weighted and wooden-spoked potter's wheel is mounted on a small wooden pivot on the ground and rotated by the potter using a stout bamboo stick against one of several points on the inside rim which are notched for this purpose. In doing so, the potter takes up the squatting position in which he will carry out the remaining work. When the wheel is judged to have attained the required momentum, the clay body is deposited on the flat wooden centre of the wheel and shaping begins.

The potter frequently dips his hand into a suspension of fine clay in water, and occasionally uses a piece of rag to smooth the pot as it is being formed. A

Opposite A potter and his family treading clay in a pit to break up lumps and mix in bajri chaff filler. In the background are kothi jars at different stages of completion.

Opposite A potter and his wife working as a team to make water-pots.

short length of string is used to sever the clay shape from the wheel once the neck and rim have been properly formed.

In the next phase the sides and base are thinned to enlarge the pot by beating the outside with a wooden paddle, shaped like a table-tennis bat, against a smooth stone anvil, shaped approximately like a minature cottage loaf, held against the inside of the pot. The potter uses a set of paddles and anvils, with varying degrees of curvature, each appropriate to a given stage in the process. These will be used in different combinations depending on the type of pot being made. While the pot is being enlarged in this way, it is rested in a shallow depression in a bed of fine grey ash.

Such vessels are not usually decorated but left to dry in the shade until the potter is ready to fire them. At this point they are stacked, inverted, in a large heap and a simple but well-formed bonfire is built around and over them, with old sherds to protect the unfired pots from the adjacent layer of brushwood, to which straw and finally a nearly black layer of clay and ash are added on the outside. The latter is carried in baskets from a near-by pit. Clay, ashes and water have been thoroughly mixed in the pit which originally yielded clay for pot making.

The clay/ash layer helps this open type of kiln to retain heat for as long as possible in order to attain the required firing temperature, and prevents the combustible material from falling out of place. Firing is usually done overnight, and the results are inspected early the following morning. A winnowing tray is often used as a fan to encourage the fire in its early stages.

Kothi jars for grain storage were formerly made larger than they are today. Some potters from Ahmedabad pose in this 19th-century photograph against several huge examples.

Kothis are fired in a similar way; because of their larger size they have to be rolled or manhandled into position. In this work and in building the kiln the potter usually draws on the assistance of other members of his family, who also help to prepare the clay. The kothi is made without using a wheel at all. A rectangular slab of clay is rolled out on a length of cotton cloth and set up vertically so that its long edges meet and are joined together. The sides are then subjected to the paddle and anvil technique and a shoulder shape given to the vessel. A separately modelled rim is then superimposed and the whole unit inverted for the addition of the thick disc-shaped base. Being thicker than a water-pot, the kothi is left longer to dry in the shade before firing. If it is decorated at all, the kothi may receive a band of short, shallow impressions at the shoulder or on the rim. Most of these pots and jars are sold through merchants in Ahmedabad.

Weaving

Nearly 200 Vasna residents work daily in factories in near-by towns or in Ahmedabad itself. These are rice mills, paper mills and various cotton-processing plants. Most of those working in the latter are members of the weavers' caste, Vankars. About fifty families in the village still engage in handloom weaving. This is fewer than in the past, but there are still far more weavers than all those engaged in other handicrafts combined. For example, potters and basket-makers account for only ten families each; there are two families of carpenters; one of tailors; and four individual stone masons.

Women may be seen weaving for wages in semi-mechanised workshops in Dholka town, but in the village their role is restricted to preparing the yarn for the loom, threading the warps through the heddles, and sometimes helping the weaver to produce more complex designs as he works at the loom. Normally this is a role which a wife performs for her husband.

Little spinning is now done in the village, and none of it from raw cotton. Women spend more time winding weft threads from a spoked wooden frame on to the bobbin which fits in the shuttle. Often yarn is doubled for strength by winding from two frames at once.

The bobbin is usually rotated by using as a spinning-wheel a mounted, hand-turned, tyreless bicycle wheel, with a loop of string as a driving-belt. Traditionally, the warp threads were laid out on a 'frame', which often con-sisted of nothing more elaborate than a set of pegs fixed in the wall of the

Using reeling apparatus which includes an old bicycle wheel, a weaver's wife transfers cotton yarn from a winding frame on to a bobbin.

Only the more skilled and patient weavers in Vasna still produce relatively elaborate pachedis. This weaver keeps additional bobbins on the left with the different-coloured weft threads required.

weaver's house, and were then threaded through the heddles and the weaving comb, sometimes using the charpoy as a firm base for attachment, before being transferred on to the loom. Nowadays, however, weavers usually do not need to wind warps at all, since they obtain yarn directly from the Cotton Mills' waste warp beams, removing short and tangled lengths, then knotting on to the ends of the previous warps. This yarn is always unbleached and sized.

When yarn is bought in hanks in the market, there is more work to do. The yarn is transferred on to a rack of bobbins before being laid out on the impromptu warping 'frame' in the traditional way already described, and finally tied to the ends of the previous warp threads. Warping in this way is necessary with coloured yarn, which is unavailable from the waste warp beams of the Mills – a practical explanation of most weavers' preference for white-ground textiles.

The loom itself is of the pit-frame type. The pit, about 90 cm long and 45 cm wide and deep, allows the weaver to operate a pair of treadles or foot-boards which are connected via pulleys to the four heddles through which different combinations of warp threads pass. Each foot raises a different pair of heddles, and by quickly and conveniently altering the tie-up between treadles and heddles, the design of the cloth can be further varied. The frame itself is essentially a means of supporting the transverse elements – the arrangement of heddles and pulleys, the weaving comb (used to 'beat in' each new weft thread) and the fly shuttle attachment which allows the weaver to work very rapidly. This device consists of a pair of wooden blocks, one at each side of a narrow wooden channel along which the shuttle is free to pass between the warp threads. Each block is attached to an arrangement of cords above the warps and immediately in front of the weaver. By pulling alternately on a pair of wooden handles attached to the cords, he shifts the blocks one after the other a few centimetres from the side towards the centre of the loom. In doing so, they sharply strike the shuttle and propel it rapidly from side to side while the shed and countershed are alternated using the treadles. Warp tension is maintained by passing the ends of the warp threads around a post embedded in the floor, gathering them together and tying them to a cord which is then attached to another post near the weaver as he works so that he can slacken off warp tension as weaving progresses.

The main textiles produced in the village of Vasna are pachedis, traditional garments worn by some farmers and other communities but especially and invariably by shepherds (Bharvads) and cowherds (Rabaris). The pachedi is worn as a loincloth (dhoti), or as a simple wrap (khes), for the upper part of the body. The term pachedi is also used to refer to coarse cotton cloth in general. Ahmedabad District and Surendranagar District to its west are the main areas of pachedi weaving. In Vasna about 60 per cent of weavers produce only pachedis; of the remainder, half produce plain cloth (khadi), which is made of mill-spun yarn purchased from the Gujarat State Handloom and Handicraft Development Corporation. The same organisation buys back the completed cloth for sale at fixed prices through its shops. The final 20 per cent of weavers produce both pachedis and khadi.

Even the most elaborate pachedis are relatively simple as Indian weaving goes, and most of the work in weaving them is extremely monotonous. Only the more skilled and imaginative weavers choose to make the more interesting *bori* pachedis, with bold-coloured borders and small triangular motifs which are created using laid-in (discontinuous) supplementary wefts, a technique locally termed *urchett*.

A pachedi consists of two main parts: a 'body' area, usually white, occasionally coloured, in simple plain weave; and the ends (*cheda*), which carry the pattern in simple float weave. The 'body' and white zones of the cheda carry a narrow warp stripe 1 cm in from each selvedge. The cheda pattern consists of a series of more or less broad transverse bands of dense colour separated by narrow stripes of contrasting colour, and other, wider zones of white or the ground colour, sometimes with smaller motifs. The cheda, which is deliberately exposed to view when the pachedi is worn, conveys information about the wearer's status, caste, age group, regional affiliation and sometimes personality. In general, the more colourful designs are worn by younger men, while older people prefer black, white and maroon. Smaller motifs, incorporated into the cheda by weaving and sometimes by embroidery, may include stylised flowers, chains, drums, fans, temples, the toran or grain (*dana*).

The pachedi is also a utilitarian garment. The risk of its tearing across the warp during use as working attire is reduced before weaving begins by grouping several warp threads together, at intervals of about 25 cm, so that they pass through a single heddle leash and between the same pair of teeth in the weaving comb. This strengthening feature, called *nav dori*, indicates the specialised character of the pachedi, despite its visual simplicity and the relatively low level of technical skill required to produce it.

The Vasna weavers are tied to a specialised market which is reliable for the time being but conservative in its taste. Pachedi weaving is on the decline, and pachedi wearers are unlikely to be able to pay more for these clothes in compensation. On the other hand, the looms used in Vasna are poorly suited to the production of other kinds of cloth, being in general too narrow, and would be prohibitively expensive for local weavers to adapt or replace. Among some younger weavers, however, there is a move to diversify what they produce; but a co-operative society, which would give them greater control over buying and selling, has not yet been organised.

Vasna: the past

The influence of the past on the present of Vasna can be described here only as an outline of its major features. Simply, we can say that the basic form of Gujarat society was shaped in the remote past and was then adapted in various ways by subsequent experience.

As well as in people's behaviour, the caste system and other aspects of local life are physically manifested in the village as material structures and artefacts. This suggests the possibility of discerning 'parallels' in the physical evidence of archaeology, indicating that local society operated in the past to some extent as it does today. Some such evidence can be found in the archaeological record, particularly from the Harappan period when settled agriculture became dominant in the region, but it cannot be interpreted too far. We are then left with a set of possibilities or probabilities, but not certainties, about the extension into the present of elements or patterns of extant culture from the remote past.

For later periods there is documentary evidence of those aspects of regional trade and other activities which contemporary writers thought worth recording. While this does not shed much light on as small a place as Vasna (at least until the nineteenth century), it does suggest the character of the regional economy in which such villages participated. It also emphasises the importance of the relationship between the village and the city, in this case, Ahmedabad, as the key to local economic integration.

The Harappan legacy

The cultural tradition identified by archaeologists as 'Harappan', which is characterised by the emergence of settled agriculture and urbanisation, probably endured as long in Gujarat as anywhere in western India. This complex was linked with the Indus Valley Civilisation and does not fade from the archaeological record until well into the first millennium BC.

Available evidence from Gujarat indicates that Harappan settlements were sparsely distributed, and it is possible that pastoralists, with their own earlier traditions, occupied the intervening territory and were not only engaged in economic exchange with the settled communities but were also implicated in commerce between settlements. Despite regional differences in its expression, the Indus–Harappan complex, lasting for perhaps two millennia, provided conditions for the entrenchment of a distinctive system of relations between urban communities, rural peasants and pastoralists.

Several aspects of contemporary Gujarat find parallels in Harappan times: methods of house-building, pottery-making techniques and the use of water-pots, the form of the bullock cart, the use of cosmetics such as kohl, the special importance attached to cows, the probable religious significance of some form or forms of 'mother goddess', the importance of foreign trade, the cultivation of rice and wheat, and the occupational specialisation of areas within villages.

Some further continuities are suggested by comparing both archaeological evidence and contemporary village life with early texts; post-Harappan Vedic literature, for example, provides linguistic clues to the origins of some cultural traits. From such secondary sources, the earlier Harappan or even pre-Harappan cultures may be credited with many of the cultural features which were perpetuated into the future. For instance, we learn from a later text, written in the second century BC, of rectangular zoning and strong gate-houses in town plans; such features call to mind not only the layout of Indus Valley cities but also the pol/khadki arrangement of historical and contemporary Gujarat. Similarly, textual sources indicate the continuity of what has been a major demographic feature of Gujarat: the restriction of the mass of the population in the villages, while urban centres functioned mainly for trade and centralised religious and political administration. The extension of the city as a habitat for more than a small élite is the result of economic changes only within the past 200 years or so.

There is, however, a general point about cultural continuities which must be made in order to avoid the misunderstanding which can arise when stating the obvious. Clearly, the present of any society develops out of its past and, as we have seen, the present way of life in Vasna is marked by certain disincentives to change. One prominent archaeologist has remarked that in order to learn more about Harappans it is not enough to dig; we must know more about existing Indian village life. This is because the systematic relationships which order the archaeological record may have included aspects of social life suggested by what can be studied in villages today. Such similarities arise not from any 'defect' in village culture but from resistance offered to some kinds of change, especially by the way the caste system operates. In some important respects village life has been subject to change all along: for example, the emergence of certain cults, focused on local female deities, has been a process of ritual innovation accompanying other, long-standing religious affiliations. Similarly, patterns of work been adjusted to new opportunities by becoming more or less specialised, while the basic technology has remained largely unchanged.

Against this background the idea of isolated elements of culture surviving from the past like fossils is unacceptable. Continuity in any aspect of a cultural system presupposes continuity in the way the system operates. An extant instance of, say, an 'early' kind of ceramic technique therefore demonstrates that the conditions for its existence can recur; but its role in ceramic technology, or in local material culture generally, may not have continued unchanged.

Production and trade before 1630

The great famine of 1630–3 marks a significant break in the economic history of Gujarat. Two centuries earlier political independence ushered in a period of steady economic growth, which reached a peak in the late sixteenth century. By the time the economic devastation of the famine was overcome, the character of trade and production had changed. Not until the nineteenth century was the economy moving again, and only within the last fifty years has it barely begun to realise its potential.

This is the context in which past generations of weavers have worked at their looms in Vasna. Living only thirty kilometres from Ahmedabad, for a long time one of the greatest textile centres in the whole of India, they were drawn into a network of trade and export. Output was almost certainly at a higher level, and a far greater variety of textiles were woven in the villages during the sixteenth century than today. As we have seen, weavers constitute a significant part of Vasna. The history of Gujarat's handicraft economy, based on textiles, is therefore directly relevant to the history of the village.

The key to understanding the development of this economy is the distinction between two systems of production and distribution: on the one hand, the

A carved, inscribed memorial stone (*khambha*), perhaps 200 years old. Apart from commemorating an historical event, about which there is no local consensus, such a stone may be used for invoking the spirit of an ancestor to secure support for a contemporary undertaking, like a marriage. As with other aspects of local material culture, the khambha is a legacy of the past but is taken for granted and may be used actively in the present.

production of goods for use in the villages or towns by the mass of the population, always supplied locally, but also to some extent traded further afield in India or abroad; on the other hand, the production of luxury goods for an élite market, either domestic or foreign. There has always been a contrast of scale between these kinds of production, which has played a large part in determining the course of regional economic development.

The allocation of specialised labour and resources to cater for the ruling class and for external trade was already far advanced when the Gujarati sultans imposed their own selective patronage on crafts during the fifteenth century. From early times Gujarat was geographically well-placed to trade with the Arab world and inland with other parts of the sub-continent.

Before the entry of the Portuguese as aggressive competitors of local merchants for the receipt of Gujarati commodities in the sixteenth century, a significant commerce was maintained over tremendous distances. Traders from the Near East, South-East Asia and the Far East were attracted by the quality and variety of merchandise available through the Gujarati ports of Surat and Cambay. At the beginning of the seventeenth century the English and Dutch became involved in Gujarati trade in an unprecedented way, setting up trading posts ('factories') in the ports and other centres to initiate orders and supervise supplies. In all of this trade, with Europe and elsewhere, nothing was more important than textiles, although a great variety of other goods were also traded. The textiles themselves included coarse and fine printed and painted cottons ('calicoes'), silks and embroideries. Later, Europeans particularly coveted saltpetre, a key ingredient of gunpowder, as their own rivalries grew noisier in the seventeenth century.

The main point about this trade is that it proves the existence of broad-based production, of both mass-utilitarian and minority-luxury goods, especially textiles, for a long period of Gujarat's history. Only the former were for local use, but both kinds were exported. The trade in cheap cotton cloth, partly for the home market but mainly for profitable re-export, was the mainstay of English commercial involvement.

The stepping-up of trade through the Dutch and English was to stimulate further the specialisation of labour in the towns and villages. Not only were consecutive technical operations now shared between different groups, but more of the craftsman's time became devoted to weaving. It was often economically more rewarding to become a full-time weaver or dyer than to combine either with farming.

This specialisation in production was accompanied by the emergence of a larger and more influential community of traders and entrepreneurs, the majority of them Hindus, at least at the lower and middle levels, whose strength lay in the co-ordination of rural production by means of buying and selling in ports and towns. The system of craft economy which they articulated was an integrator of rural and urban life.

These developments certainly left at least some, probably the majority, of craftsmen materially better off, but there is no doubt that the middlemen secured the greatest reward. They began to accumulate capital which, if it had been invested in new equipment by a merchant class increasingly conscious of its own interests, would probably have raised the economy to a stage where it might have competed directly with later imports from England. But capital was neither accumulated in large quantities nor used in this way; the merchants, from various communities, remained for the most part ideologically committed to the existing political system and more aware of their traditional family obligations than of their common economic interests. The social appears to have dominated the economic – the influence of caste again; and the result was the eventual domination of local economy by the superior mercantile organisation of Europeans.

For the village artisan most work continued to be done at home. There was some movement of population into the towns and cities, and a setting up of urban workshops resembling regular factories, but these concentrated on luxury production and accounted for only a small part of the total craft output geared to trade. Even today at least some Ahmedabad textile mills recruit among specific communities to provide workers in certain phases of the production process which are traditionally allocated to them. Under such conditions it is not surprising that the labour force has been relatively docile. This situation is directly comparable with the organisation of production in the sixteenth century. The labour force was then also divided, between different villages and different areas. It was an arrangement which automatically assisted the entrepreneur, or the political ruler out to augment his own income, rather than the artisan. That was a disadvantage which the weavers may have eventually overcome had not the famine intervened.

Production and trade after 1630

Particularly by abandoning cultivation in favour of handicraft production, large numbers of rural Gujaratis probably made themselves even more vulnerable than they might have otherwise been to shortage of food. As it was, three years of unprecedented famine decimated the rural population. The primary producers, the cultivators, lasted as long as their meagre food stocks; the specialised weavers probably perished even faster. The impact on craft production and trade was immediate and lasting.

There were two main results: first, European traders had to look elsewhere in India for the products which they needed. It was the cheaper, village-made material which had become unavailable as the looms lay idle. At the same time, the world market was changing and a new demand arose for cheap calicoes to be sold in West Africa and the Caribbean; but Gujarati designs were now being imitated elsewhere in India, in response to European attention, and by the time local textile production had even partly recovered, its privileged trading position had been undermined.

The second effect of the destruction of the rural labour force was the emergence of luxury production as a relatively more significant factor in post-famine trade. Cheaper textiles continued to be produced; but in the villages, whence they mainly derived, weaving did not recover as quickly as in the towns and cities, where luxury production was concentrated and where it depended on a much smaller labour force. A larger proportion of urban craftsmen probably survived the famine in any case.

Another factor was the state of the market. Most rural production was for domestic use; and consumers as well as producers starved to death or emigrated to other parts of the country. Luxuries were only ever produced for an élite which, in Gujarat, elsewhere in India and abroad, survived or was unaffected by the famine. Demand from this quarter was therefore felt much earlier than from the peasantry, and craft organisation was better placed to meet it. The domestic craft economy has been overshadowed ever since by the often magnificent products of specialised craftsmen.

It remains to mention only three other developments which are relevant to the later economic history of Ahmedabad and its hinterland. First, the local specialism of both village and city weaving meant that this part of Gujarat largely withstood the tremendous impact of the English Industrial Revolution in the eighteenth century. In many parts of India the influence of the Lancashire power looms was devastating as cheap cotton textiles flooded the market, so that, in the words of the 1834–5 report of the Governor-General, 'The bones of the cotton-weavers are bleaching the plains of India'. The English mills could not compete with the main kinds of textiles woven in central Gujarat – coarse dyed and printed cottons from the villages and printed silks and

BROTSCH

The conspicuous wealth and commercial activity of Gujarati towns clearly impressed early European visitors even if their descriptions, and the images projected by their illustrators, lack objectivity. Even without the Chinese architecture and other spurious details the port of Broach was an important place in the seventeenth century.

brocades, produced by some village and urban weavers. Luxury production was relatively immune to factory competition, and the local élite constituted a reliable market as their cultural conservatism resisted the pressure towards westernised dress which found more response in other Indian cities. Profits acquired by Gujarati merchants from trade in raw cotton and in opium, as well as in luxury textiles themselves, had the same effect of buttressing this system of production.

Central Gujarat survived Lancashire to create the basis for Ahmedabad's own textile mills in the late nineteenth century, of which the first was opened in 1861, three years ahead of the railway linking the city to the port of Cambay. After the Famine this was the second disruption relevant to village weavers. It was the mills, directly competing against them for the mass domestic market, which were to have a greater impact on Vasna and other villages in the hinterland and further afield.

The British had taken over the administration of Ahmedabad in 1817 and imposed restrictions on mill production to protect the home industry. These began to be lifted only in the 1930s. Even under these conditions, as a contemporary gazetteer reports, by 1879 coarse cotton cloth from village handlooms had been largely superseded by that produced in the mills of Ahmedabad and Bombay.

From the last third of the nineteenth century onwards Gujarat's own power looms have forced village handloom weaving to rely on a narrow, traditional, shrinking market for such fabrics as pachedis, which are not produced at all by the mills, or on the wider market for khadi or other textiles in which the mills can afford some competition.

The future of weaving in Vasna therefore looks uncertain. Even if co-operative societies are set up, they may have come too late. If the mills have maintained a largely benevolent attitude towards the village weavers, this may be simply in recognition of their economic insignificance. Paradoxically, it may be the sign of a brighter future for Vasna when the mills start getting tough.

Not far from Vasna a 'Gobar' gas plant provides a group of poor farmers with fuel and fertiliser from animal dung and household refuse. This improvement on the wasteful practice of using dung only for fuel needs a recognition of common interest and a readiness to alter fixed routines if villagers are to benefit from it on a wide scale.

Conclusion

In common with much of rural India the token village of Vasna combines old with new. On the one hand many physical features of village life remain traditional, such as architecture, some household equipment and craft technology, but it is social relations, arranged in an occupational hierarchy buttressed by the concept of ritual pollution, which offer the strongest resistance to change. The relative stability of the caste system has created the conditions in which, within the limits of local technology, craft skills could attain a high level of refinement. On the other hand the supply of electricity, the prospects of reliable harvests, the proximity of an expanding industrial city and the villagers' growing involvement in the wider world have set in motion a process of change whose future course is hard to predict. But it seems likely that in the next two or three generations the traditional material conditions and craft products of village life will be transformed along with the social relations that they reflect.

Further reading

Part One From village to city in ancient India

AGRAWAL, D. P., *The Archaeology of India*, London and Malmö, 1982

ALLCHIN, Bridget and Raymond, *The Birth of Indian Civilization*, Harmondsworth, 1968

ALLCHIN, Bridget and Raymond, *The Rise of Civilization in India and Pakistan* (forthcoming)

HIEUN TSANG, *Buddhist Records of the Western World*, 2 vols., trans. Samuel Beal, London, 1906

SANKALIA, H. D., *The University of Nalanda*, Madras, 1934

SANKALIA, H. D., *Pre-history and Proto-history of India and Pakistan*, Deccan College, Poona, new edn. 1974

SHARMA, G. R. (*et al.*), *Beginnings of Agriculture*, Allahabad, 1980

WHEELER, R. E. M., *The Indus Civilization*, 3rd edn., Cambridge, 1968

Part Two Vasna: village life in Gujarat

Anthropological Survey of India, *Peasant Life in India: A Study in Indian Unity and Diversity*, Memoir no. 8, Calcutta, 1971

Census of India, 1961, *Volume V: Gujarat* (various parts), Delhi, Manager of Publications, 1965

FISCHER, Eberhard, and SHAH, Haku, *Rural craftsmen and their work: Equipment and Techniques in the Mer Village of Ratadi in Saurashtra, India*, Ahmedabad, National Institute of Design, 1970

GOPAL, Surendra, *Commerce and Crafts in Gujarat, 16th and 17th Centuries*, New Delhi, People's Publishing House, 1975

IRWIN, John, and SCHWARZ, P. R., *Studies in Indo-European Textile History*, Ahmedabad, Calico Museum of Textiles, 1966

JAYAKAR, N. D. PUPUL, *The Earthen Drum: An Introduction to the Ritual Arts of Rural India*, New Delhi, National Museum, 1980

LANNOY, Richard, *The Speaking Tree: A Study of Indian Culture and Society*, London, 1971

MALIK, S. C., *Understanding Indian Civilization: a Framework of Enquiry*, Simla, Indian Institute of Advanced Study, 1975

PRAMAR, V. S., *Wooden Architecture of Gujarat*, Ph.D. thesis, M.S. University of Baroda, 1980

Index

Page numbers in italic refer to illustrations.

abstinence (sexual) 62
acrobats 80
agriculture 55, 57, 58, 88
Ahichchhatra 14, 41
Ahmedabad 55, 57, 58, 59, 64, 67, 82, 84, 85, 88, 89, 91, 92
Ahmedabad District 79, 87
Ajanta 46
Allahabad 42, 71
alms 81
aluminium 71
Amaravati 43, 45, 46
Andhra Pradesh 45
Antichak 49
appliqué work 73
Arab world see Near East
Archaeological Survey of India 26, 43
Arthashastra 44
Aryans 36
Ashoka 13, 42, 44, 45
Atranjikhera 39

bajri 58, 80
Baluchistan 18, 24
bamboo 63, 72–3
Bangladesh 13, 49
banian 77
Bannu 32
banyan-tree front cover
Barhut 45
Baroda 58
basket-makers 60–1, 62, 72, 73, 85
basketry 72–3, 73
Bavla 82
beadwork 73
beakers 71, 72
bedding 69
Belan River 15, 18
Benares 14
Bengal 49 ff.
Bhagalpur District 48
Bhagwanpura 34, 35–6
bhangis see basket-makers
Bharvads (shepherds) 54, 77, 87
bicycles 81
bicycle wheel (used in spinning) 85
Bihar 48, 49, 57
Bina River 48
black and red ware 39
blankets 69, 77
bobbins 85, 85, 86, 86
Bombay 58, 92
bori pachedi 87
Brahmins 62, 81
Brahmi script 42
brassware 61, 67, 71
bricks 63; see also houses
British 92; see also English
Broach 92
brocades 92

Buddha 44, 46
Buddhajnanapada 49
Buddhism 46, 49, 51
bullock carts front and back covers, 80, 81, 82, 88
bullocks 59
Burma 51
Burzahom 20–3, 35

calendars 65, 73
'calicoes' 90, 91
Cambay 90, 92
cap, Ghandi 77
capital accumulation 90
Caribbean 91
carpenters 85; see also woodwork
carts 71; see also bullock carts
cash crops 58
caste 90; solidarity 80; system 55, 61
chakla 73
change, social and economic 55, 62
chapatis 71, 75
chappals 77
char 71
charpoy 60, 68, 69, 69, 86
Chenab River 35
chests (storage) 69, 70
childbirth 75
children 61, 63, 89
Chopani-Mando 15–17, 18, 19
chula 64, 67
cities 13, 14; life in 58
clay 70, 72, 82
cleaning 75
clothing 69
coinage 41, 42
communications 57, 58, see also transport
containers 65, 69, 70, 71, 75
continuity see cultural continuity
contraception 79
cooking 60, 67, 69, 72, 80; see also food
co-operatives 62, 87, 93
cosmetics 88
cosmic order 80
costume see clothing, dress
cots see charpoy
cotton 58; raw 92; processing plants 85
cow-dung 63, 69, 75; cakes 55
cows 75, 81, 88
cradles 63, 68, 69, 74
crockery 70, 71
cultivation cycle 58–9; see also agriculture
cultural continuity 88, 89
Cunningham, General 26, 43
cupboards 70; see also containers

Dadheri 34–5
dancers 80
Deccan 35, 36, 38

deities 73, 80
dhabalo 77
Dharmapala 49
Dholka 59, 64, 79, 82, 85
dhoti 77, 87
dishes 71, 75
Diwali 80
doab 39
domestic space, allocation of 64, 67
doors 59, 64, 65, 65, 66, 69, 70, 81
dowry 69
dress 77; see also clothing
dunghills 75
Dutch 90

earthenware 61, 71, 72; see also pots
eating 60; see also food
economics 89
economic specialism 91
education 58, 62, 79
elections see politics
electricity 73
electric light 60, 63, 73, 75
embroidery 73, 90
English 90; see also British
English Industrial Revolution 91
entertainment 80
entrepreneurs 90
Eran 48
Europeans 59, 90, 91

factories 85
fairs 78, 79
famine 57, 70, 89
Far East 90
fertilisers 55, 57, 59, 75
fertility 75–7
festivals 62, 71, 78
fire 72
floors 63, 63, 70, 75
fly shuttle 86, 86; see also loom, weaving
fodder 58, 82
food 63, 70, 75–7, 80, 81; preparation and storage of 69
footwear 77
fuel 55
funerals 62
furniture 64, 65, 69, 70

Gandhi 62, 79
Ganesh 73
Ganganagar District 26
Ganges Civilisation 41
Ganges River 13, 39, 71
Gangetic Iron Age 39
gateways 61
gestures 64
ghagra 77
ghee 70, 75
Ghod River 36
goathair 77, 77
'Gobar' gas plant 93
Gopala 49
grain 73; storage jars see kothi
gram see pulses
Great Bath, Mohenjo-daro

27–9
Greek and Roman contact 44
Gujarat 13, 24
Gumla 25
gunpowder 90
Guptas 48

Harappa 24, 26
Harappan culture see Indus Valley Civilisation
Haribhadra 49
Harijans (Untouchables) 57, 62, 80
harvest festival 81
Hastinapur 14, 40, 41
hawkers 80
head-gear 77
hearth 60, 64, 69, 72, 75, 80
heddles 86; see also looms
Hiuen Tsang 50, 51
Hindus 57; religion of 46
Holi 80
hospitality 62
houses 59, 59, 60, 60, 63, 64, 93
house-building 88
hurricane lamps 73

images (religious) 69, 73
Inamgaon 35, 36–8
industry 62
Indus River 25, 26
Indus Valley Civilisation 24–34, 41, 88, 89
inequality 58
innovation 89
insecticides 57, 58, 59
Iron Age 39 ff.
irrigation 57, 59

Jainism 46
Jammu 35
Jamuna River 39
Java 51
jewellery 69, 78
Jorwe ware 36
jugglers 80
Jumna River 71

Kalibangan 24, 26 ff., 32
Kandahar 44
Kartikeya 79
Kartik Swami see Kartikeya
Kashmir 18, 20, 38
Kasia 14
katodan 69
Kausambi 14, 17, 41, 42, 43
Kautilya 44
khadi 87, 93
khadki 59, 59, 60, 64, 75, 89
khatco see charpoy
khes 87
Khairpur 25
kites 80, 81, 81
Koldihwa 18, 20
Kosala 44
Kot Diji 25, 36
kothi 67, 69, 70, 82, 83, 84, 84

labourers 56, 59
lamps 60, 73

Lancashire 92; power looms 91
land ownership 57, 58; use 55, 57
leather-workers 62
Lewan 32
lighting 69, 73; *see also* electric light
lime plaster 61
lintels 73
loincloth *see dhoti*
lofts 64, 65, 67
looms 60, *63*, 86, *86*, 87
Lothal 33

Magadha 44
magicians 80
Mahabharata 44, 79
Mahadaha 17
Mahagara 18–20, 22, 25
mahajanapada 13, 44
Mainamati 49
majuh see chests (storage)
Makar Sankranti 80, 81
Makran Coast 25
Malwa ware 36
Manasa 52
mand 70, 71
Manda 34–5
Manu 44
manure *see* fertilisers
marketing 62
marriage 62
mass communications 58
Mathura 41, 48
matka 82
Mauryans 44, 45
Mehrgarh 18
Meluhha 32
memorial stones (*khamba*) 89
merchant class 90
Mesolithic 15
millet 58
mills, cotton and textile 73, 86, 91, 92, 93
millstone 61, *61*
mirror-work 73
Mohenjo-daro 24, 26–9, 31, 32
'mother goddess' 88
mud (in house-building) 61
mung see pulses
musicians 80
Muslims 57

Nalanda 48, 49, 50–1
Near East 90
Neolithic 18 ff.
Nepal 44, 51
newspapers and magazines 58
Noh 40
Northern Black Polished ware 40
North-west Frontier Province 25, 32

occupational specialisation 88
occupations 62

Oman 33
opium 42
ordo 65, *65*, *67*
Orissa 44
otlo see veranda
outsiders 64

pachedis 77, *86*, 87, 93
paddle and anvil (technique in pot-making 84, *84*
Paharpur 49
Painted Grey Ware 35, 36, 39–40
painting 66
Pakistan 13, 18, 21, 24, 26, 29, 31
Palas 48, 49 ff.
Paleolithic 15
Pandava brothers 79
paper mills 85
paraffin stove *67*
parsal 67
partitions 64, 65, 69; *see also* walls
pastoralists 88
Pataliputra 13, 44
patara see chests (storage)
Patels 57, 63
Pattikera monastery 49
patronage 90
photographs 67, 69, *74*
pilgrimages 62
pit houses 21, 22, 37
plaster 63
pol 89
politics 58, 62
pollution *see* ritual pollution
pond *see* tank
population, movement to towns, cities 91
portraits 67
Portuguese 90
post-box *81*
pot-covers 71
pot-making 82–4, 88, 89
potters 60, 62, 72, 82, *83*, *84*, 85
potter's wheel 82, *83*
pots 61, 71, 82
poverty 64
Pratapgarh District 17
prestige 70, 75
prices 58
prints (religious) 67, 69, 73, *74*
production (two systems) 89, 90, 91
prosperity 77
protein 75
pulses 75
Pune District 36
Punjab 25, 35, 38, 39, 40
purity (ritual) 62–3, 72

quilts *67*, *68*, 69, 70

Rabaris 77, 87
radio 63, 69
Rahman Dehri 25
railway 82, 92
Rajasthan 13, 24, 26

Rajghat 14
rainfall 57
Rajputs 57, 63, 82
Ramayana 44
rank *see* caste
Ravi River 26
religion 46, 57, 62, 89
reservoir *see* tank
rice, and cultivation of *56*, 57, 75, 80, 88; mills 85
Rigveda 36
ritual pollution 60, 62–3, 69, 73, 75
rituals 62
Rohri Hills 32
roofs 63, 67

Sabarmati River 57, 79
Sahiwal District 26
saltpetre 90
Sanchi 45
Sangam literature 44
sanitation 61
Sankissa 17
Sarai Nahar Rai 17
Saraswati River 35
sari 78
Sarnath 45
Saurashtra 25
school *56*
seasons, seasonal time 58–9
security 65, 69
sexual activity 75
sherds 84
shops 57, *81*
shuttle *see* fly shuttle
Sibi District 24
silks 90, 91
Sind 25, 26, 36
Siva 34, 79
soak-pits 61, 67
soil, saline 57
Somapura monastery 49
Sonkh 45
South-East Asia 44, 90
spinning 85
Sravasti 14, 41, 44
starching wool 76
steel 71; stainless 72
stone masons 85
storage 65, 67, *67*, 70, 85, 86; *see also* containers
streets 64
sugar 75, 80
Sukkur 32
sultans, Gujarati 90
Sungas 45
superstition 73; *see also* deities
Surat 90
Surendranagar District 87
surpluses (food) 70
sweepers 62

Tamils 44
Tamluk 47
tank (pond, reservoir) 61, 75
Tara 51
Tarakai Qila 25
teaching *see* education
technology 89

Terai 44
textiles 70
thali 40
theft 60, 69; *see also* security
threshing *56*
Tibet 49
toran 3, *65*, 73, *74*
tractors 57, 82
trade 88, 89, 90
tradition 55
transport 55, 62, 81, 82, 92

Untouchables *see* Harijans
urbanisation 88
Uttar Pradesh 18

Vaisali 14
values, social and religious 80
Vankars *see* weavers
Vasna 55
Vatrak River 79
Vatsas 44
Vautha 79; fair at *78–9*
Vedic literature 89
vegetables 75, 80
vegetation *see* agriculture
ventilators 64, 69
veranda (*otlo*) 59, 67, *68*, 69, *74*
Vikramshila monastery 49–50
villages 13
village settlements 55, 59
Vindhyas 15, 21

walls *55*, 59, *66*, 70, 72, *81*
warping 86; frame 85, 86
warp tension 87; *see also* looms
washermen 62
washing 61, *61*
water-buffaloes 59, *59*
water, drinking 61, 75
water-pipe 72
water-pots *67*, 82, *83*
water, symbolic aspect 61
Waziristan 25
weavers (Vankars) 57, 62, *63*, *76*, *77*, *86*, 89
weaving 57, 85, 86, 87; comb 86, 87
'Welcome' 73
wells 57, 59
West Africa 91
wheat 58, 75, 80, 88
White Huns 48
windows 60, *63*, 64, 69, 73, *75*, *81*
winnowing fan (tray) 73, 84
winter solstice 81; *see also* Makar Sankranti
woodwork *64*, 67, 70
wool *76*, 77
workshops 91
writing 33–4, 41–2

yard 59
yarn 85, 86